HEALING the WEST

HEALING the WEST

voices of culture and habitat

Jack Loeffler

Museum of New Mexico Press
Santa Fe

Project director: Mary Wachs
Design and production: David Skolkin
Cover design and illustration: Bette Brodsky
Manufactured in the United States of America
10 9 8 7 6 5 4 3 2 1

Library of Congress Cataloging-in-Publication Data
Loeffler, Jack, 1936-
Healing the West : voices of culture and habitat / by Jack Loeffler.
p. cm.
Comprised of two major sections extracted mainly from documentary radio series and sound collages produced by the author since 1984.
ISBN 978-0-89013-520-4 (clothbound : alk. paper)
1. Indians of North America—West (U.S.)—Government relations. 2. Cultural property—Protection—West (U.S.) 3. Habitat conservation—West (U.S.) 4. Human ecology—West (U.S.) I. Title.
E78.W5L55 2008
323.1197078--dc22
2008012744

Museum of New Mexico Press
Post Office Box 2087
Santa Fe, New Mexico 87504
www.mnmpress.org

*This work is dedicated to the seventh generation of those who follow . . .
with hope and love.*

↠ **H**EALING THE WEST is a many-faceted
stream of human consciousness respond-
ing to the leitmotif of homeland. It is comprised of two major sections extracted
mainly from documentary radio series and sound collages that I have produced
since 1984. The first section, "The Spirit of Place," focuses on the relationship of
indigenous cultures to respective habitats located in the western United States.
The second section, "Moving Waters: The Colorado River and the West," is
drawn in part from a radio series of the same title and addresses the role of the
Colorado River in development of the Southwest over the last century. I have re-
vised and augmented both of these sections with selections from other radio and
sound-collage productions to provide the reader with a flavor of the history of the
West spiced with highly differentiated cultural points of view. This nonlinear ap-
proach is designed to create a sphere of reference regarding human habitation of
a landscape whose main characteristic is aridity. Although I have written a fair
amount of introductory and connecting narrative, the main body of this work is
a practice in aural history comprised of excerpts of recorded interviews that I
have conducted over a period of nearly forty years that have been digitally dupli-
cated and included in my aural history archive to be donated to the Palace of the
Governors History Museum in Santa Fe, New Mexico.

This book is one of four components of a larger project funded by a grant
from the Ford Foundation, which includes the digital duplication of a large portion of my aural history archive, the training of Native American and Hispano
community scholars in the practice of aural history, and production of a fifteen-

part documentary radio series, entitled *The Lore of the Land*, which has been nationally distributed to Community Public Radio stations via satellite, Public Radio Exchange, and CD production. The overall project was administered by Dr. Sue Sturtevant, director of Statewide Partnerships for the New Mexico Department of Cultural Affairs, and sponsored by the Museum of New Mexico Foundation. The various aural history projects that have provided excerpted narrative for this book were funded in part by grants from the National Endowment for the Humanities, administered by Dr. Craig Newbill, director of the New Mexico Endowment for the Humanities; the National Endowment for the Arts; and the New Mexico Department of Cultural Affairs.

As is revealed in the pages that follow, my abiding interests are the preservation of natural habitat, the relationship of culture to habitat, the role of biodiversity in spawning cultural diversity, and the contribution of cognitive diversity to survival potential for the human continuum in the coming centuries or even decades. I have presented material both intellectually and intuitively rendered from within communities of practice and cultures of the interviewees. Scientific and historic perspectives are interspersed with intuitions brought into focus through the lens of mythic vision. In my own mind, they are not mutually exclusive but rather interdependent and vital for the evolution of consciousness.

This book is offered with humility in the hope that some of the seemingly disparate pieces of the great puzzle begin to integrate.

JACK LOEFFLER
Los Caballos, New Mexico

T HIS IS A BOOK of hope, of twirling metaphors reflecting our intuitions of times past, present, times to come, reflections of the mythic process at work throughout the American West. The fabric of this book is woven of myriad voices of those who have shared with me their stories, their thoughts, their understandings, sometimes disparate, sometimes in accord. To all of these people whose voices shall ring forth and be recognized in the pages that follow, many of whom are my closest friends, I am grateful.

I am also grateful to those whose voices do not appear, yet who have been of incomparable help to me in this project: my dear friend Sue Sturtevant, who has never missed a beat along the trail; my buddy Craig Newbill, who is indefatigable; Estevan Rael-Gálvez, a true friend of clear mind and great insight; Suzanne Jamison, who is adept beyond belief; my pal Claude Stephenson, who stands among the finest of men; the remaining sacred coterie of The Lore of the Land—Jim McGrath, Enrique Lamadrid, Rina Swentzell, and Stewart Udall; the old gang of the Black Mesa Defense Fund, both living and dead; to Tom Aageson, Jean Peters, and Nancy Brouillard, all friends who kept the energy flowing; to Mary Wachs, Anna Gallegos, and the superb staff at the Museum of New Mexico Press; to Yvonne Bond for all her help with transcriptions; to the Ford Foundation, National Endowment for the Humanities, New Mexico Humanities Council, Christensen Fund, New Mexico Department of Cultural Affairs, New Mexico Arts, Museum of New Mexico Foundation, Bureau of Land Management, National Park Service, National Forest Service, Natural History Museum of New Mexico,

Center for Arts of Indian America, Ruth Mott Fund, Western States Art Federation, Tucson Pima Arts Council, Smithsonian Institution, Western Folklife Center, and the National Endowment for the Arts, each and all of whom funded components of the last forty years of my enthusiastic adventures with recorder and microphones; to the living watersheds of this planet and those biotic communities who have sung to me through the darkness and into the dawn; and especially to Katherine, my wife and compañera of my lifetime, and to our daughter Celestia Peregrina, my esteemed production assistant of many years, and her husband, Michael French—

Thank you all and everyone.

Conflicting

Ideologies,

Spiritual Chaos

⇒ I T IS AUTUMN in the high desert country of the American Southwest, this enormous span of landscape through which I have wandered for half a century. By human reckoning, the hundredth meridian separates the verdant East from the arid West, and though I was born near the banks of the Ohio River, I was lured westward early on to pursue the adventure of life in a much less humid habitat where one could see mountains a hundred miles distant and listen to the echoes of drummers whose bones have long since turned to dust. This is a mythic landscape, sparsely vegetated, where wildlife yet abounds ever wary of the shadow of a hawk, the scream of a mountain lion, the footfall of the human hunter.

Indeed, this has been the homeland for hunter-gatherers for thousands of years, and even though the last five centuries have been witness to enormous changes wrought by many waves of human immigration from distant continents, the lore of this land harkens back through countless generations wherein mythic history is recalled in oral tradition and renderings of art carved or painted on canyon walls. The mythic histories of many cultures reveal facets of collaboration between human inhabitants, myriad fellow species, and local deities. And as the cycles of the seasons roll through time in space, ceremonial song and dance continue to honor the spirit of place ever recalling the lore of the land.

However, the voice of indigenous culture has been diluted over the last centuries, first with the coming of the Spaniards in the sixteenth century, followed by eastern Americans wending westward in the early nineteenth century. Newcomers brought with them a religion dominated by belief in a single transcendental deity intent on subsuming the local spirit beings, which resulted in secularization of homeland and paved the way for turning habitat into money.

Conflicting ideologies have resulted in a form of spiritual chaos within the lives of native peoples that is barely perceptible to relative newcomers. This spiritual and cultural chaos places the rest of the western biotic community in grave peril. Indeed, my own first vision of this mythic landscape was illuminated one dawn in the glare of an exploding atomic bomb in a remote corner of the Mojave Desert of what is now southern Nevada. On three occasions in 1957 I was witness to the violent application of nuclear physics to the regional habitat, a blinding light that fired my own consciousness. At the time, I was a young jazz musician drafted into the U.S. Army as a trumpet player in the 433rd Army Band. The shock of witnessing the testing of nuclear bombs in that low desert habitat in the Colorado River watershed while playing "The Stars and Stripes Forever" honed my mind to the necessity of continuously evaluating the mores of the culture into which I was born. It gradually became clear to me that habitat comes first, and that human cultures within habitat, to be successful in the long term, must be biased in favor of the biotic communities in which they share membership. Their systems of mores must include a perspective of habitat as the nurturing entity that sustains them both physically and spiritually. This seems such an elementary notion, but somehow it has largely vanished from the greater fabric of American monoculture.

Many cultures indigenous to the intermountain west of the United States are still visible due both to extreme aridity and to their relative isolation, even in the face of vigorous human encroachment from without. While Southwestern watersheds are modest in yield, indigenous cultures have necessarily adapted to the carrying capacities of their habitats, exhibiting models of cultural conduct that coincide with the flow of Nature. This is not to imply that indigenous cultures have refrained from trashing their habitats. Indeed every human community that remains fixed in place profoundly affects the surrounding biological and sometimes even geophysical nature of the environment. But it is a matter of degree. A Hopi village affixed to a mesa top for a thousand years is still capable of self-sustenance, compared with communities of more recent provenance where the inhabitants rely almost entirely for sustenance from without and would be bereft should mechanized transportation break down depriving them of food and other "necessities."

A fundamental difference between the Hopi residents of Third Mesa and the residents of nearby Page, Arizona, is one of cultural attitude. Whereas the Hopis hold the land in great reverence and perform annual cycles of ceremonials celebrating their spiritual ties to homeland, the residents of Page owe their arrival to the construction of the Glen Canyon Dam, an enormous concrete plug that stoppers the once-mighty Colorado River, and the Navajo Generating Station, a coal-fired power plant that spews electricity and noxious fumes throughout the West.

But more on this later.

Gradually, I transplanted myself into the high desert country of northern New Mexico. I rolled into this habitat like a tumbleweed, and now only rarely wander out of range of the intermountain west. Little by little, I shifted out of the mode of jazz musician (in 1962, I was the only one that I knew of north of Route 66) and turned my attention to listening to and recording the music and lore of traditional peoples. I became a hunter-gatherer, my recorder and microphones being the tools of my hunt, the media of radio, sound collage, and albums becoming the modes of sharing what I gathered. Even now, I wander throughout the West and Mexico visiting and befriending fellow humans born into cultures whose languages are of different phyla than my own, and whose mores are sometimes difficult to comprehend. Gradually I have come to the realization that indigenous cultures are constituents of their respective habitats, which in part shape cultural evolution.

Concurrently, I became an environmental activist as I watched my newfound ranging land come to be pillaged and plundered of its forests, its waters, its subterranean resources, including coal, natural gas, oil, uranium, and the like. And as developers and extractors rammed their way into the desert hinterland, I witnessed not only the ravaging of biotic communities and landforms but also the expunging of indigenous cultural self-consciousness from the flow of Nature.

Thus, throughout my adulthood, I've come to defend the rights of indigenous peoples to practice their cultural traditions in accordance with their respective ideologies, and their rights to protect their homelands against the juggernaut of so-called Western civilization. I've also gained great respect for the clarity of the lens of mythic perspective, for it is through myth that culture intuitively defines itself and cultural homeland is geo-mythically mapped. It is through intuition that we sense our intrinsic and spiritual relationship to the flow of Nature. It is through science that we attempt to understand the relationship of the microcosm to the macrocosm, the fact of the presence of life on this planet, the birth and history of our universe that is currently the largest ecosystem our modest collective consciousness can fathom. I've encountered collaborations between scientists and indigenous culture bearers that have resulted in exponential increases in understanding the relationship of indigenous human culture to habitat. This "consilience" is truly an invaluable lesson in the application of cognitive diversity.

I'm convinced that cognitive diversity is vital to the well-being of the human species, and that it is spawned through the marriage of biodiversity and cultural diversity. I regard centralization as a grim mistake, and believe that we should perceive from within watersheds rather than from within geopolitically defined boundaries, a challenging ideal considering the state of overpopulation that our species has visited upon the planet.

Over the last four decades I've been privileged and honored not only to have listened to the music and lore of many indigenous peoples but to have recorded it as well. Subsequently I've archived a body of aural history that contains thousands of songs and hundreds of interviews with anyone willing to speak his or her mind. There are recordings of habitat wherein one may hear the chorus of inhabiting biota. And there are recordings of individual species of birds, mammals, reptiles, and even insects. It is from this archive that I've produced radio programs, sound collages, albums, books, and essays in a modest personal attempt to "put it back," to reinvigorate cultural self-esteem, to elicit a renewed sense of meaning of individual and cultural indigeneity to habitat far more real than any paradigm manifested by the economic-political-military complex that presently dominates much of world culture.

In the book that follows, I've drawn from the narrative of certain of my radio and sound-collage productions, reviewed and rewritten articles and lecture notes, written new material, and woven the following text in the hope of elucidating a perspective founded on the premise that if life has a purpose, individual and collective consciousness lie at the heart of it. It will only be through evolving human consciousness and the celebration of cognitive diversity that we may yet wend our way through the threatening forces that jeopardize not only our species but also the entire biotic community of our planet, Earth.

PART I

The Spirit
of Place

T HE FAIREST THING we can experience is the mystery. It is the fundamental emotion which stands at the cradle of true art and true science. He who knows it not and can no longer wonder, no longer feel amazement, is as good as dead, a snuffed-out candle. It was the experience of mystery—even if mixed with fear—that engendered religion. A knowledge of the existence of something we cannot penetrate, of the manifestations of the profoundest reason and the most radiant beauty, which are only accessible to our reason in their most elementary forms—it is this knowledge and this emotion that constitute the truly religious attitude; in this sense, and in this alone, I am a deeply religious man. . . . Enough for me the mystery of the eternity of life, and the inkling of the marvellous structure of reality, together with the single-hearted endeavour to comprehend a portion, be it ever so tiny, of the reason that manifests itself in nature.

—ALBERT EINSTEIN
The World As I See It

ORAL TRADITION is intrinsic to indigenous cultures. It is through oral tradition that stories and songs convey cultural memory and reflect the nature of human presence in the home habitat. The mythic process is a tremendously powerful means through which culture communicates with the spirit of place. It refines intuitive processes and aligns spiritual coordinates within the realm of homeland. The local deities are present and alive, and the fellow creatures who share homeland—coyotes, eagles, bears, hummingbirds, rabbits, buffaloes, beetles, ants, grasses, trees, shrubs—are themselves regarded as sacred within the geography of habitat. The Earth is the most sacred of all, with her mountains, forests, deserts, and waterways clearly defining the geo-mythic map of homeland.

With the advent of the written word, history emerged as a linear perception of human presence on the planet. The Old Testament of Hebrew tradition is both a chronology of ancient tribes and a shift in mythic perspective wherein the local spirits were taken out of Nature and a single anthropomorphic transcendental god was relocated to some heavenly realm available to humans through priestly intervention, or after death.

Prehistoric humanity, whose presence on the planet gradually emerged as Homo sapiens between 150,000 and 200,000 years ago, developed points of view, some of which are still to be found among traditional peoples who continue to celebrate Heaven on Earth. As Paul Shepard wrote [in Coming Home to the Pleistocene]:

Prehistoric humans . . . were autochthonous, that is, "native to their place." They possessed a detailed knowledge that was passed from generation to generation by oral tradition through myths—stories that framed their beliefs in the context of ancestors and the landscape of the natural world. They lived within a "sacred geography" that consisted of complex knowledge of place, terrain, and plants and animals embedded in the phenology of seasonal cycles. But they were also close to the earth in a spiritual sense, joined in an intricate configuration of sacred associations with the spirit of place within their landscape.

These "sacred associations with the spirit of place" linger on within those with the strength of cultural character to withstand the zeal of outsiders who would foist their beliefs in a transcendental god on indigenous peoples, thus paving the way for secularizing the landscape.

Many years ago, I acquired a map of the contiguous forty-eight United States that reveals the boundaries of both geophysical divisions of the landscape as well as provinces therein. By looking at this map, I found that where I live near Santa Fe is a point where three distinct geophysical divisions of the continent coincide—the Rocky Mountains, the central plains, and the intermountain west. There is only one other similar point in the United States, and that lies in what is now known as Illinois where the central plains, the Ozark Plateau, and the coastal division conjoin. These are powerful points of convergence, major ecotones where wildlife habitats overlap, and the spirit of place presents a mosaic of wondrous complexity. They elicit major geomantic considerations.

Through the western window of my studio, I look out over the intermountain west, that vast expanse of landscape that lies between the Rocky Mountains to the east, and the Sierra and Cascade mountain ranges to the west. This region extends from just south of the Canadian boundary to deep into Mexico. It is the most arid landscape in North America, and is drained by three river systems, including the Columbia–Snake, the Colorado–Green–San Juan, and the Río Grande–Pecos–Conchos.

Because of the aridity of the region, it has been the last part of the United States to suffer overdevelopment. Descendants of the original inhabitants still pursue traditional lifeways throughout, and the presence of the sacred still prevails in spite of the incursions of extractors of natural resources and developers, and their men in government.

In 1995, with a great deal of help from my friend, folklorist Elaine Thatcher, and a grant from the Ruth Mott Fund administrated by Elaine, who was then working for the Western States Arts Federation, I was able to travel throughout the intermountain west and beyond conducting interviews, recording wildlife, and deeply absorbing the flow of Nature in order to produce a thirteen-part radio series entitled *The Spirit of Place*. I camped along the way in the back of my old Chevy pickup truck, and marveled at the loveliness of the ever-changing landscape. I filled my mind with the sounds of habitats, listening in stereo, thus displacing the mono mode of linear thinking to which I fall prey if I don't take great care. I watched as countless mountain ranges appeared on the horizon; joyfully suffered the heat of North America's four deserts; skinny-dipped in watersheds that drained into the Pacific Ocean, the Atlantic Ocean, and the Sea of Cortés; and luxuriated in the wisdom of fellow humans who allowed me to record conversations with them.

By autumn of that year, I returned to my homeland with a palette of sounds from which I would create sound collages pursuing my art form. During the following winter, I produced the radio series, and through the help of my good friends at KUNM Community Public Radio in Albuquerque, the series was distributed around the nation. What follows is a transcribed portion of the yield of that great adventure. I've included excerpts from the dozens of interviews I conducted as I roamed the American West from one end to the other. I visited many friends and gathered stories and reflections from folks whose cultural fabric is woven from myth and indigeneity to habitat, as well as commentaries from bioscientists, writers, activists, and iconoclasts, all of whom provide deep insights into the lore of the land.

Life originated in its simplest form, on our tiny planet at least, more than 3.5 billion years ago, or so scientific evidence suggests. However, about 540 million years ago, there was a true explosion of life which resulted in what biologist Edward O. Wilson called "the Big Bang of animal evolution." Over the next 475 million years, ever-evolving life forms burgeoned the delicate biosphere in great spasms of abundance only to be thwarted by major episodes of extinction wrought by volcanic activity or inundations of asteroids, which resulted in tremendous rents in the fabric of biodiversity. The last major episode of extinction occurred about 65 million years ago, when the age of dinosaurs came to an end. Since that time, mammals have come into their own. Through accident or predilection, our own species has come to exist, hopefully to become conscious enough to remain.

Alvin Josephy was both one of my dearest friends and one of America's most eminent historians. In 1984 he addressed the coming of early man to the Western Hemisphere.

ALVIN JOSEPHY: "It now looks, very much, as if man began to come, if he hadn't already come, around 35,000 or 40,000 years ago. [Many archaeologists and paleontologists think that early man entered North America about 16,000 years ago.] Now, just at that time, Neanderthal man still existed in Eurasia. And Cro-Magnon man, the successor of the Neanderthal man, also existed. He was coming into more and more prominence. The two were still on Earth. The Neanderthal man was still on Earth. Now, that was a very early period. There is no evidence that Neanderthal man got here [North America]. In fact Cro-Magnon man was more developed. He had learned how to make a higher stage of tools and weapons and so forth. He was more advanced technologically than the Neanderthal man. And that is perhaps one of the reasons why he persisted and Neanderthal man died out. With his more advanced abilities and knowledge, he was able to expand and migrate into areas where no man had been before, or is known to have been before, into the less hospitable parts of the world, the colder regions. He got up into Siberia, and was able to venture across what was then the so-called Bering land bridge when it appeared. And Cro-Magnon man, Homo sapiens, got across into the New World, and it looks like about 35,000, 40,000 years ago. Now, who those people were we don't quite know. They came from Asia somewhere, and probably in small groups they began their expansion over the two Americas. And they are the oldest ancestors of American Indians in the Western Hemisphere."

This gradual migration was occurring during the Pleistocene epoch, or Ice Age. It was during this long epoch that we attained species-hood and basically became who we are today. In *Coming Home to the Pleistocene* the brilliant ecologist Paul Shepard wrote:

"In that archaic past we perfected not only the obligations and skills of gathering and killing, but also the knowledge of social roles based on age and sex, celebration and thanksgiving, leisure and work, childrearing, the ethos of life as a gift, and a meaningful cosmos."

Indeed, we perceived life as a great mystery, and as cultures gradually evolved as their respective habitats evolved, regional landforms became sites of great mythic relevance. Existence within the homeland was given depth of meaning when viewed through the lens of mythic perspective.

Gary Paul Nabhan is an ethnobotanist and co-founder of Native Seed Search of Tucson, Arizona. He is an award-winning author, whose many books include *Gathering the Desert*, *The Desert Smells Like Rain*, and *Cultures of Habitat*. He is a strong advocate in behalf of traditional cultures, and has long recognized the role of folklore, folk song, and oral history in the preservation of the spirit of place.

GARY PAUL NABHAN: "To restore the land, we have to re-story it. And I think this is a key element: that whether the stories come to us through poetry or oral history, odyssey, and other epic narratives, or whether it comes to us through some combination of music and performance, these ritualized stories tell us who we are and relate us to the land in a way that reminds us of that relationship. It reminds us in a way that is not just a head-way but a heart-way and a gut-way to remember our relationship to the land. That we are part of the land community. Its story is in a very real sense our story. And people who forget the story of their relationship to the land are the people most vulnerable on this planet.

"Bill Kittridge, in his book *Who Owns the West?*, says that it is not simply a fact that individuals can forget their story, their autobiography—that whole cultures are doing it now. And he feels that in the American West the Anglo-American culture has forgotten its story, or determined that its original story of the frontier epic is now obsolete. It is not guiding us anymore, and that we need to find a deeper story. How can we find those very ancient connections to the land, and build upon them so that we have a bedrock-solid sense of place?"

i.

The Columbia Plateau extends between the northern Rockies and the Cascade Mountains. Geophysically it was formed by the spread of dark volcanic lava. Herein is situated the watershed for the Columbia–Snake–Yakima river systems, which join and flow westward, emptying into the Pacific Ocean. Many cultures have been sustained by this landscape and the rivers that nurture it. The Clearwater River is a tributary of the Snake River. The Nez Percé Indians are indigenous to this region. Today, their reservation is located in west-central Idaho near the Oregon boundary.

Mylie Lawyer was a Nez Percé elder who made her home in Lapwai, Idaho, for many years. Her mind was a reservoir of Nez Percé stories and history. I spent a wonderful day with Ms. Lawyer as she spun yarn after yarn. She spoke of Coyote, the archetypal trickster whose presence is vital to Indian peoples throughout the West and beyond.

Mylie Lawyer: "Coyote was coming up the river. There are always stories of Coyote going up the river and Coyote going down the river. Different things happened to him going up and coming down. And he was going up the river because he was going to go to Buffalo Country. It was cold and the river was frozen. There was ice everyplace. So that would indicate kind of like an ice age. He walked along and there was a frozen deer horn or antler sticking out of the ice. He stepped on it and it hurt him. So he went limping along and he saw these shelters along the side of the river on the bank. So he went up there, and there was this girl, and family. And he told them what was wrong. And she said, 'I will fix it for you.' So she fixed his foot. And he said, 'Oh, let me be a handsome man.' So he turned into a really good-looking young man. And he was going to try to marry this woman. But her grandmother told them, 'That is Coyote. Be careful. That is Coyote.' Anyway, it is a long, long story. But what fascinated me always, it starts out, 'It was cold. And there was ice everyplace. And that river was frozen. And Coyote stepped on this deer horn that was sticking out of the ice.' And to me that always means that it must have been a long, long time ago when there was a lot of ice here."

Fisherfolk and other hunter-gatherers have lived throughout the watershed of the Columbia–Snake–Yakima river system for many thousands of years. Long ago they were able to develop intertribal cultures of practice that sustained them without destroying their collective habitat. Archaeological evidence suggests that cultures have been in place in this watershed for 12,000 to 15,000 years. One of the great gathering points was Celilo Falls in the Columbia River where salmon abounded.

Rock art appears in this region, some of which reflects cultural recollections from mythic history. Jeanne Hillis is a lore gatherer who has lived much of her life in this region. She recalls the legend of She Who Watches.

Jeanne Hillis: "There is a petroglyph over a little west of Horse Thief Lake called She Who Watches. And it is supposed to be a lady that sits there. And she watches everybody.

"One time Coyote was walking along the river. And he decided that he was going to find the wisest person on the river. He went from village to village and he would ask, 'Who is the wisest person in your village?' When he was satisfied, he would move on. He came to this little place along the Columbia River. It was a lovely place because there were little sloughs where they could catch waterbirds. There were fish. There were enough roots and tules and plants that they could use. So people stayed there, and they had a little village there.

"Coyote came by and he said, 'Who is the wisest person in your village?' And someone said, 'Oh, it is that old lady who lives up on the hill. She is good to us.' He went a little farther and said, 'Who is the wisest person in your village?' 'It is that old lady. She has been here a long time. She knows what to do.' So he went from person to person. Finally he went up to talk to the old lady and he said, 'Is it true? Are you really the wisest person in your village?' And she said, 'Well, I try to be. I try to see the people get along. I try to see that parents are good to their children. I try to see that people have enough to eat. I try to be.' He said, 'All right. I guess you are the wisest person in your village.' And with that, he took her and he threw her up across the cliffs, and he said, 'There. You can watch over your village forever.'"

The Columbia River watershed yields more water by far than any other watershed in the contiguous United States west of the Continental Divide. The mosaic of human cultures has flourished there for many millennia, sustained in large measure by the bounty of salmon yielded throughout the river system. The presence of salmon figures deeply in the perspective of ancient cultures that continue to subsist in the watershed.

In my travels, I met Ed Edmo, who is descended from Shoshone, Bannock, Yakima, and Nez Percé Indians. He has lived much of his life near the Columbia River in The Dalles, Oregon. As a youngster, he learned to fish for salmon within the native tradition using nets called dips, a style of fishing that has been practiced there for thousands of years.

ED EDMO: "I started fishing, actually, when I was seven years old. I caught my first fish. It was a little Jackson. It was about a foot and a half. When a person fishes, and he misses the fish, then we kids get a chance to fish for it. So my father missed the fish, and I took a dip and caught the fish. I was seven years old. I remember my father and I have the picture somewhere. We got a picture of that. We brought the fish home and ate it.

"Then I used to fish around Celilo on the rocks at different places. And when I turned thirteen, I got to fish with my uncles and my father. I had four places to fish. I had one with my uncle by the falls, one with my uncle at the channel, and one with an uncle in Chinook Rock, and another one on Chinook Rock. It was kind of like a distant uncle. And we would all take turns. I learned how to make a net, and fish with a net. And I used to sit there and fish with the men when I was thirteen years old. All my cousins were playing, and I was fishing, making a living. It was kind of interesting."

Sharon Dick is a fisherwoman who lives on the Yakima Indian Reservation. She maintains a fishing platform on the Columbia River where she catches and dries salmon after the traditional fashion of her people. In the course of her lifetime, she has witnessed a spectacular decrease in salmon populations in the Columbia River watershed due to construction of massive dams, pollution from pesticides and nuclear waste, and unchecked offshore salmon fishing. She fears that should the current trend continue, salmon will finally disappear from their home watershed.

SHARON DICK: "Our first food is the salmon. It is important for us to have salmon. Every Sunday we are supposed to eat salmon. It is our way of life to thank the creator on Sunday and eat the traditional foods. And that is a lot of salmon. The way I see the numbers declining, it is really scary for me. The Indian people used to walk so close to Nature. The Columbia River was clean-flowing water at one time. They said you could see all the way to the bottom it was so clean. I think way back then, when the fish were in great numbers, they went to their streams, and they were hearty fish. And now they are not. I think the dams warm up the water. A fish can't go, like we can, from the hot sun into air-conditioned rooms. They can't do that. Their body temperature has to adjust before they can move. When they come into that mouth, they got one thing in mind. They are going to spawn. And then they have to fight all these things. Different elements and things, and water temperature. And they are coming a long ways. When they leave here, they are just little-bitty things, and yet they go out there and they feed. And they come back. And the big salmon that comes back, he has got a real battle from the mouth of the Columbia clear up to Wishram, fighting all the different dams."

Indeed the damming of western waters has wrought havoc with wildlife at every turn. Pesticides and other forms of pollution have diminished salmon and many other species. Allen Pinkham is a Nez Percé elder whose role is to communicate the point of view of his people to government agencies in order to forestall continued destruction of habitat, which results in endangerment and extinction of species.

ALLEN PINKHAM: "If you relate your body parts to individual species that have been eradicated from this North American continent . . . if you relate the Peregrine falcon to your little finger, and the buffalo to another finger, or maybe the sockeye salmon up to your elbow, when would you stop sacrificing your body parts to save a species?

"If you relate your body to your Mother Earth and the environment, then that is another way of thinking. If you do that, you will start to understand the way Indians feel about Mother Earth. Let's not sacrifice one species for another. Let's restore their habitat. Let's restore the species. Because if you relate that to body parts, when are you going to say, 'No more extraction, utilization to extinction of species?'"

Mr. Pinkham expressed his deep concern for the fate of Indian peoples whose traditional lands have gradually been subsumed by interlopers whose superior numbers and military might have forced the Indians to gather on tiny reservations. Often several tribes are forced to share the same reservation, thus diluting their cultural points of view and lifeways.

ALLEN PINKHAM: "A lot of tribes have been lost, or their identity has been lost because they have been absorbed into other tribes. There are over forty tribes in the Columbia River basin. Some of those are lost, and some are on to reservations now, and they are called a group. Like the Caldwell reservation would have fourteen different bands of tribes. And I can't name them all. But then you go to the Yakima reservation and there's another fourteen bands.

"After the treaty times, after 1871, when they said they were not going to have any more treaties, they created an executive order reservation. And some of our people that were Nez Percé went to these other reservations and were absorbed. They were very closely related to us. They all depended upon the river system. Like the Palouse people, the Cayuse, Umatillas, Warm Springs people, Klickitats, Chinook, you know, all the way down to the mouth of the Columbia. And I think they have the same values we do.

"Some of it has changed dramatically because they don't have a land base. And it is hard to have a culture without a land base. That is what a lot of tribes are trying to do, get a land base, so then they can restore their culture and some of their cultural practices. We have done fairly well, but not perfect. And I don't think we will ever get back to our traditional way of living because that is a completely different kind of lifestyle than what we are in right now. And besides, some of the resources that we relied on aren't there anymore.

"That is the other thing—I am working with the Forest Service in restoring some of those species that we relied on so we can take up our traditional practices again. There are a few people that do that now, but not as a tribal entity do we do it because some of the resources are just not there. You have to have the species there and the habitat there to do that. If you bring back the gray wolf, the grizzly bear, Peregrine falcon, and all those species, that is bringing back those things that we valued in those old days. So without that occurring, our lifestyle is going to be changed dramatically. And some of it may be lost. Another way of preserving culture is to preserve species."

Many of the geophysical elements of the Columbia River watershed are threatened or have already been eradicated. People who are unfamiliar with regional terrains fail to comprehend the mythic significance of landforms to indigenous peoples. Geo-mythic mapping is unfamiliar to anyone who has lost the ability to sense the mystery inherent in landscape. Pat Courtenay Gold is a Wasco Indian who rues the obliteration of landforms that marked the mythic coordinates of her people's homeland.

PAT COURTENAY GOLD: "Our legends are based on rock formations because the basalt rock was all volcanic. There were different designs from the hot lava. The rock formations defined certain images. A lot of our legends were based on those images. Since the dams were built, it is all gone. Celilo Falls is gone, and all the rock formations are gone. Our legends that were tied to these landforms still have meaning to me because I can remember them. But the younger generations, they can't tie them to those visual memories. They can hear the songs in the legends, but they can't tie them to our physical culture. To our location. To our land base. I think that one of the problems is that they don't have that strong tie."

Allen Pinkham tells a part of the Nez Percé creation myth that reveals the importance of landforms to the geo-mythic map of his homeland to his people.

ALLEN PINKHAM: "There is a monument up here that is called Heart of the Monster. It is up the Clearwater River a way, about sixty miles. Coyote was beckoned one time. Another animal came to him and says, 'There is a big monster up in the Kamiah Valley, devouring all the animal people.' This is before human beings had come about. And Coyote said, 'Well, I will go up and see what I need to do to this monster. So he got ready a nice little bag, and he got pitch and soot. And he got flint for knives. And he got a rope. So he went. And he would holler at the monster.

He said, 'I hear you are devouring all the animal people. You can't devour me, because I am not going to let you.'

"So he would tease the monster. Then finally the monster raised his head up over the prairie, and looked at Coyote. He was on the other side of the prairie. And so they talked back and forth. And Coyote just teased him. And then finally the monster said, 'I am going to suck you into my belly.' And Coyote tied himself to the mountain. And the monster tried to suck him. And Coyote would just come to the end of his rope, and he would just stay there. The monster kept trying to suck him in.

"Finally Coyote said, 'Well, I am going to go in.' So he takes out one of his knives and cuts the rope, and goes into the monster's mouth. And he gets inside, and he sees all the animal people. Some are just bones. And some are dying. And some are still alive and want to get out. So he told all the animal people, 'I am here to save you. I am going to kill this monster.' And then Grizzly Bear growled at him. Coyote said, 'Well, what are you growling at me for? I come here to save you, to get you out of here.' And Grizzly Bear growled and so Coyote pushed him with his hand, and pushed his nose. So that is why the grizzly bear has a flat nose.

"And then he walked on farther, and then Rattlesnake rattled at him. And he said, 'What are you rattling at me for? I came here to save you.' Rattlesnake rattled again. So Coyote stepped on his head. And that is why the rattlesnake has a flat head here.

"And finally Coyote said, 'Well, I am going to cut this heart down, and melt all this fat.' And they built a fire. And he started cutting the heart loose. And he cut. And one of his knives would break. So he would get out another knife. And he kept cutting. And finally he got to the last strand of flesh that was keeping the heart on. He told the animal people, 'Get ready to get out of here. Go to all the holes in the body. The nose, the mouth, the ears, and the hole under the tail. You all wait there. Because when this monster takes his last breath, then all these holes will open, and then it will close, and you will never get out.'

"So he said, 'I am going to cut this last piece. So get ready.' So he cuts it. And the heart follows, and then the monster takes his last breath. And all the animals run out. All except Muskrat. He was just too slow. He was running out of the hole underneath the tail. And that last breath, that hole closed up on his tail, and stripped all the hair off it. So that is why the muskrat only has just a little bit of hair on his tail. He got it all stripped off, when he ran out of there.

"And then Coyote, he got out, and then he said, 'Well, what am I going to do with this monster? Well, I am going to create the human beings.' And so he would cut a body part off and he would throw it in the direction to the east. And he created the tribes. The Osage, Kutenais, the Sioux, the Cheyenne, the Shoshone-Bannocks, the Yakimas, and all the way around up north he would throw these body parts. And when they struck the ground, then human beings would be created.

"And then he finally got done, and he says, 'Well, there is no human being right here. We will have to create people here. Nice beautiful valley. Nice place to be.' So he wiped his hands of the blood. And as those drops of blood struck the earth, people sprung up. And these were Nez Percé. And he says that these people will be strong people, kind people, able to live with their neighbors. Good human beings. So this is where they will be. Right here. And he said, 'Well, I will need to mark this place.' So, he took the heart and he put it in the ground. And it looks like a heart. And the nice round hill. And it is about eighty, ninety feet high. And there was a liver also. He put the liver over there. And he laid it there and said, 'I'll leave this here as a landmark so people will know that the Nez Percé were created here. And this will mark the site of the creation of Nez Percé.' So that is the story."

According to the legends of many peoples, there was a time when animals could speak among themselves. The interaction between humans and other species, and the folk tales of the Indian peoples, provide great insight into the minds of those who perceive themselves as part of, rather than separate from, the greater biotic community. Among many Indian peoples, the influence of Coyote was boundless.

Ed Edmo's mother was a Yakima–Nez Percé, while his father was a Shohone-Bannock. He was born near Fort Hall, Idaho, in 1939, but his family moved to Celilo, Oregon, in 1940. Mr. Edmo is a true lore master. Here he lets us know that Coyote has a lascivious streak that was the bane of many a maiden.

ED EDMO: "Coyote was the great inventor. Whatever Coyote wanted he would have it. Coyote said, 'Boy, I would sure like to be with these two young Swallow girls. They are sure pretty. I would like to have them hug me and kiss me. That would really be nice.' So he said, 'I am going to change myself into a baby.' So he changed himself into a little baby. And he got into this little basket, and went down the river in the basket, crying like a little baby. And these two Swallow girls, they picked this little baby up. 'Look at this cute little baby.' And these other Swallows said, 'No, don't touch that baby.' She said, 'Why?' 'That is Coyote.' 'No.' She said, 'Yeah,' and took the blanket off and said, 'Here is his partner.' And he had his pubic hair. And he said, 'Changed himself but he couldn't change his partner.'"

Sophie George is a Warm Springs Indian who recounts a Coyote story that prepares Indian maidens for adulthood and also could indicate that Coyote may well have been the scapegoat in affairs of the heart.

SOPHIE GEORGE: "There was this beautiful meadow, and this young girl was walking by. Coyote stopped the young lady and he said, 'You know, there is a beautiful flower out in the meadow. It is red.' He said, 'When you see this flower, you sit on this flower.' And this young girl never experienced life. So when she was walking along, the Coyote had left her and she saw this beautiful flower. And she sat on it like the Coyote told her. And then Grandma says, 'And you know what happened?' And I said, 'What?' And she said, 'She had a baby.' And I used to wonder, 'What kind of flower did she sit on?' And it wasn't until I got married that I understood the story. But the thing of it was, I never knew when Grandma was telling me stories that it was preparing us for life. I used to always be scared about red flowers because I thought I don't want to have a baby."

Animal stories abound in every Native American culture. They reflect the affinity that exists between Indians and other creatures, or between different species in their respective habitats. Ed Edmo tells the following story.

ED EDMO: "Little Porcupine wanted to get a buffalo. And he said, 'I am going to go hunt buffalo.' And there are no buffalo right around his area. But he had to go hunt the buffalo. So he was sitting one day, sharpening his quills. Stick it back and get another one, sharpen it, stick it back, get another one. 'Whatcha' doin'?' Porcupine says, 'I am going to go hunt buffalo.' 'Where are you going to go?' 'I am going to go out towards Montana and find me a buffalo.'

"So he took off. He was going down the road. The little porcupine. And all of a sudden he saw a buffalo chip. He stopped to look at the buffalo chip and said, 'Gee, buffalo chip, how long you been here?' 'I have been here a month,' the buffalo chip said. 'Well, at least I am on the right track. Been here a month? Which way did they go?' 'They went that way.' OK, so Porcupine takes off that way. Away he goes. Pretty soon he ran into another buffalo chip. 'Buffalo chip, how long have you been here?' 'Oh, I have been here about two weeks.' 'Which way did they go?' 'They went that way,' the buffalo chip said. So away he goes. Every time he sees a buffalo chip he asks the buffalo chip, 'How long ago have the buffalo left?' You know, two weeks, one week.

"Then he got there one day, and he said, 'Dang! Boy, this buffalo chip looks pretty good. He was steaming hot.' And this porcupine, he touched it. 'Hey. It is still warm. Hey buffalo chip, how long have you been here?' He said, 'They just left me.' He said, 'Where did they go?' 'They are across the river over there.'

"So Porcupine goes down by the river. And he sees the buffalo, all of them standing, wishing he could cross the river. So he yelled, 'Hey buffalo, come help me cross the river.' And this old skinny buffalo says, 'Oh, you want me to help you?' 'No, I don't want you. I want that fat one over there.' Another one hollered, 'I'll help you.' 'No, I want that fat one there.' So that fat one says, 'Want some help? Yeah. I'll help you.'

"So the buffalo walks across the river. He says, 'OK Porcupine, jump on my back. I'll give you a ride across.' He says, 'No. The flies. You shake the flies, I'll fall off and drown.' 'Well, how can I get you across?' He said, 'Swallow me.' 'OK.' So the buffalo swallowed him. So away he goes. And Porcupine says, 'Buffalo, how far are we?' He said, 'I just started to cross the river.' And Porcupine is in there just sitting there in the stomach. And he said, 'How far are we now buffalo?' And he said, 'About in the middle.' And he waited and waited. 'How far are we now?' And he said, 'Oh, I am about ready to get out.' And he said, 'Well, how far are we?' And he said, 'I am just getting out of the water now.' And Porcupine sat there and said, 'Where are we at now?' And he said, 'I just got out, I am ready to get on the land.' He waited for a while and said, 'How far are we now?' He said, 'I am on the land now.' So the old porcupine just shook himself all over, and all his quills went in his [the buffalo's] stomach and killed him. And he crawled out of his mouth. And that is how he gets his buffalo.

"That is an old story. I heard that when I was a little kid. I heard that. When the buffalo chip talks, and he points, he uses his lips. And you know old people, old Indians, when they point, they do that. You ever notice that?

"Long time ago, years ago, way back when the animals used to talk, they had Possum. Possum had a great big humongous fluffy tail. And he would really flaunt that tail around. He would go to dances, and dance. And always show this fluffy tail. And he said, 'Look at my beautiful marvelous fluffy tail.' He would brag about the tail, and he would swoosh it around. People got so where they didn't like to see him because he would brag so much about his tail. And he was a pretty animal. He would dance and shake himself: 'Look at my marvelous, beautiful fluffy tail.'

"So later on during this one powwow they had, he was in there showing off. These people said, 'Well, in morning when he gets tired, he'll go to sleep, we'll fix him.' So early morning, he got tired, lay down, and went to sleep. They called the Indian doctor to come by, and said, 'We'll fix him.' So he said magic words to him, took his tail, and went like that [rubbing his hands together] to his tail. Put something on his tail, all the way to the end. And pretty soon he had a long tail like a rattail. And he said, 'We'll fix his nose too.' So they said magic words to his face. And his nose got plain so he wouldn't be handsome. So there he was.

"He woke up that morning, and old Possum, he got up. And there, he had that nose and the big long skinny tail. And he went out there and he started dancing. Showing off his old beautiful, marvelous fluffy tail. He was dancing, and looked down, and there was this old stick sticking out. His own tail. He saw that and he got ashamed. He took off. And when he took off he looked back to see who was watching him. And when somebody would come to him he would fall down. Pretend like he was asleep. That is how possums are today. That is how possums came to be."

Generally, traditional Indian peoples are spiritually attuned to their homeland in a way that is difficult for non-Indians to comprehend. Their sense of belonging to habitat is a tremendously powerful force that provides them with the intuitive perspective to perceive the numinous quality that pervades Earth and her offspring. Land and life are sacred and recognition of this contributes to the sort of spiritual refinement that I have frequently encountered among Native American elders whose sensibilities coincide with the flow of Nature through their homeland.

Allen Pinkham tells the story of a young Indian and an animal spirit guide.

ALLEN PINKHAM: "The men were coming back to the camp after hunting. And this young boy was in camp and he was told, 'You go take these horses back to the pasture.' So the boy did what he was told. He took the horses and put them in the pasture. And when he was out there, it started snowing. And he became lost because the tracks were covered up. So he was wandering around there trying to find his way back to the camp. And he finally stopped and saw that he had snow all the way around him, and he couldn't find his way. And so he stopped. And he looked back towards the backside of him. And he seen five men coming. And they walked right by. And the last man said, 'Come with me.' So the young boy said, 'Oh, they must know where they are going.' So he started following the five men. So he followed them, and then he came to his camp. And they said, 'Well, there is your camp right over there. You go on down there.' So he said, 'Well, OK.' So he went down towards camp and he looked back. And those five men turned into five wolves. So the five wolves showed him the way back to his camp. And then they left him and went on their way. So that is the spiritual connection we have with species. And wolves is one of them."

For thousands of years, indigenous peoples of diverse traditional lineages have inhabited the greater watershed of the Columbia–Snake–Yakima river system. Undoubtedly their forebears learned a great deal by observing their fellow species, and little by little a collective body of lore was assembled, which was shared by many indigenous humans who may have spoken no common language or dialect. However, fishing, hunting, and gathering were common to everyone, as was an enduring sense of affinity with Mother Earth upon whose good health they continue to rely for sustenance, both physical and spiritual. Their environment provided for them. And through ingenuity and perseverance they developed skills for gathering and preparing foods, constructing shelter, and fashioning artifacts.

Jaime Pinkham is a member of the Nez Percé Tribal Council. He is greatly concerned about continued impoverishment of habitat due to industrial pollution and the shortsightedness of federal agencies. He believes, as do many Indian people, that Nature thrown out of balance can only result in disaster.

JAMIE PINKHAM: "When we think in terms of the natural environment, I think the greatest concern is the loss of species. We are losing some diversity and some balance in the ecosystem. Probably the most notable would be the salmon. Now, on the heels of the salmon, we are looking at the steelhead—the declining runs of steelhead in this country. And it is important to these communities because of physical sustenance, but also when we look at those species, there is the spiritual sustenance that they provide. Our activities reflected our understanding of the changes in the land, the changes in the water. And we knew where to move when it was time.

"For example, to harvest salmon wasn't just a harvesting experience, but it was also a spiritual experience, the celebration and the honoring, giving thanks to Nature and to Creator for these gifts. The spiritual part of it also is important to a healthy community. So the health of the community is dependent upon a healthy Nature and spiritual health as well. I think the tribe's been working hard in their efforts to restore the fisheries to this area. But it is a difficult task. We look at the changes in the river. A gentleman once told me that when you change the river you change the fish. When you change the fish, you change the Indian people. And you could look at the changes to our community with time, changes in our eating habits, changes in our livelihood. Whereas we used to gather for these celebrations to honor the return of the salmon, we are losing that reason to celebrate because the runs aren't as plentiful as they once were. People are beginning to look at other means or other sources of food, and that does concern me because we used to come together in these kinds of celebrations. We need to keep working to restore these fish runs so we will continue to have cause to celebrate.

"I guess even more importantly, we want to help our children find reason in their future to celebrate too. I think our efforts don't stop just at the fisheries. We can look at what the Nez Percé tribe has been doing in reintroduction of other species—protecting habitat for other species that are important to us. For example, the tribe has taken a leadership role in the reintroduction of the gray wolf to most of north-central Idaho. In addition, we are working closely with federal and state agencies on protecting habitat for whitetail deer and for elk, and trying to protect the bighorn sheep populations within our tri-river area. It extends around both the river system itself and the surrounding habitat. They get their drainages of the river system. And we always see that the tie, that the reason that we want to protect that environment, because it does create a healthy physical and spiritual community for the Nez Percé."

As Paul Shepard pointed out in his provocative book *Coming Home to the Pleistocene*, we humans achieved virtually all that biologically characterizes our genome by the end of the Pleistocene epoch, the last Ice Age, some ten thousand or so years ago. Ten thousand years is one hundred centuries. If we consider that humans reproduce at the rate of about five generations per century, we are separated from our Pleistocene ancestors by about five hundred generations. Very little has changed biologically within us over that time span.

In those chilly days of yore, our species-hood owed much of our survival quotient to our ability to hunt and gather. We were (and thus remain) great tool-makers. Our sensibilities were finely honed to the flow of Nature, and we hunted and gathered our way to a level of consciousness that allowed us to extrapolate where game to hunt was likely to be, or when roots and fruits would be ripe for the gathering.

ALLEN PINKHAM: "When we talk about Mother Earth we are talking about us receiving nourishment from Mother Earth. We should be taking care of Mother

Earth, making the water pure so she can survive and not dig into the rocks for minerals and destroy her skin. Or cut the trees. It's like cutting her hair. All we need to do is start to understand why we are here and how we are connected to Mother Earth. What we call the blood for Mother Earth is the Clearwater River, the Snake River, the Columbia River. If you look in the veins of your body, you will see how it flows and goes into branches. It is the same thing with Mother Earth. Those rivers and streams are like arteries, and supply blood for her life and the things that she provides for us."

ED EDMO: "I remember in the springtime of the year, when my uncles and my dad fished, they'd bring fish up to the house. When I was nine, ten, eleven, twelve, thirteen years old, we used to carry sacks of fish up to the house to my grandmother and my aunts. And my mother and them, they all cut the fish. And they would put it in drying fish, and put it in salt, and dry them. Cut them really thin in layers. And dry them. Put newspapers in place so they wouldn't get stuck together, then put them in racks and dry them. And I remember when I was a little kid, my job was to chase the flies away. So I had a newspaper, and I would always go in there and chase the flies away all the time. And I always got the first taste of raw fish to the finished product. I was always eating on fish. In the springtime here we did that. And just before fall time. When the season was closed they couldn't sell it. So that is when they brought 'em up and they dried them, canned them. And they sat in the salt water. And we had salted salmon, dried salmon, and canned salmon. They would bring twenty or thirty sacks of fish up. Some of the sacks could only hold two fish in them too. Some of them were dragging on the ground, when I used to bring them up. And it was kind of a growing [up] thing: who could carry the most fish or who could carry the most fish in a sack all the way home without stopping."

SHARON DICK: "You catch a salmon, you cleaned the salmon. And you leave it for like about eight to ten hours. You hang it up. You let all the blood and the water come out. Then you fillet it off the backbone. Every part of the salmon, basically, is used for food, except the insides. You hang it on dowels. The red salmon you do in the shade. The red meat. And you hang it up on poles, and you get it to where it starts to dehydrate and it gets a stiff texture. And you hang it up on preferably cedar sticks. Cedar is a natural insect repellent. And then you just let the wind dry it. All you put on it is salt. You let the wind dry it. That is the red salmon. The red-meat fish. And then in the fall time, when you dry the tule stock, then you fillet the fish, and you have big racks outside in the sun. You fillet those fish, and you lay it out in the sun until it gets a stiff texture. Then you move into a smokehouse. You have smoke going on it. It stays in there like a week. Older wood is the best wood. Some of the people used to use white oak in Underwood Village. But my sister and I found that white oak is too strong. It makes good smoke, but it is really strong and it tends to make the fish taste bitter. Alder is the best."

Mylie Lawyer was born in 1912. Her mother was an Oglala Sioux, and her father was a Nez Percé. She went to high school in Lapwai, Idaho, where she was the class valedictorian. She then went college where she majored in economics. When I interviewed her in 1996, her mind was as clear as springwater, and she provided me with her recollections that reflect the tradition of the Nez Percé people within their homeland.

MYLIE LAWYER: "They had to pick certain woods because there are certain woods that would give it a bitter flavor. For instance, like cottonwood would. And they would try to get willow or alder. They never used pine. That was one of the first things the women did. As soon as they got their camp established when the men were hunting is to get the wood for smoking. Just like Archie Lawyer told them when he was trying to get the captive Nez Percé from Indian Territory. He said they were used to eating their fish and their deer meat and elk meat and their roots. That was their basic diet. They got the salmon from the river.

"My father always told me when he was a little boy, of course he had no father or no uncles or anything there. But there were two men that always took him out in a canoe. And they would go out at night. And they would build a fire at one end of the canoe, and he had to watch it. And the fish would come up to see the fire. And they would come up to the edge of the water, and they would do that in the wintertime to get the whitefish. He said they were bony. And then they fished for the salmon and trout, whatever they could get. They would do that. And then they always went for their venison and their elk. And nearly everybody went up the mountains to hunt. And the women went along and they cut and they dried their meat to eat. Then in the springtime, it began about June, the women began to dig. And they had these diggers. And they dig them [roots] up. And they get them ready, and they dry them. And it is pure carbohydrate. It is just like potato. They have one that they call *caus-caus*. They have another one they call *caquit*. It is similar to the other one. But it tastes a little bit different. And they have the bitter root. And then they have a wild carrot that is crisp and white inside with a light brown color. But it is sweet and nice. And they dry those. And that is for their winter. And then in the fall, like now, they are up to Wiap digging *camas*. And they bake that in a pit, and build a fire. And put the bear grass over it and wet it, and put their roots in it, cover it up, and for three days they keep a fire on it. Then they open them up and the roots are black. And it made the Lewis and Clark expedition sick. They all got stomachache from eating those."

Horace Axtell was born into the Nez Percé tribe in 1924. His recollections give an invaluable perspective of Nez Percé life in the twentieth century.

Horace Axtell: "We used to travel from Ferdinand clear down to south Idaho. My mother had friends down there she would go see every year. They would save her deer hides. And she would take these buckskin gloves and moccasins that she made. She would make a bunch, and then take them down and trade them for deer hides again. And they would save her a lot of other things. They would trade canned food, and things that way. We'd come back with a whole bunch of things. Every year it was like that and the same way in the fall.

"When she prepared for the winter, we used to raise wheat on that little piece of ground we had. And then when we'd harvest our wheat, she would go and have twelve sacks set aside for flour. We would never run short of flour all winter. We had a storage shed. She put it away and covered it up with canvas. And keep it free from the mice and everything. I think that all comes from the way the old people used to migrate. It is like I was talking before. The first food that comes in the spring is on the hillsides up here. And that first one is like the leader. And when the first one is harvested, we have a feast. And whatever we have left over from the winter, we put in with that first food. The different roots that we have. And different fish. Meat. Like deer meat, elk meat, moose meat. Eating animals. And berries, like huckleberries and serviceberries, and chokecherries. And we have a feast of all these traditional foods. And so that gives us like a new life for a year. Until the fish food comes again. So during our lifetime, if one should die in between the cycle of a year, when that person is getting ready to go the good place, we have a feast with all the same foods. So that is how much respect we have for Mother Earth. We say we go back to Mother Earth to become dust. We put ourselves in the ground to recycle all these good things. So the newborn will have all these things. But like I say, it is getting awfully hard to gather some of these sacred foods now. But something that we still pray for, after the beginning of the New Year, we start praying for the new foods to come. Every year. Sing songs and pray."

ED EDMO: "When a person dies in the family—your father, mother, brother, sister—the old-timers used to cut their hair. Cut their braids out. They still do. My brother cut his braids off since my father died. You can attend, but you can't participate in the powwows for a year. And after a year, you have a giveaway dinner. And after the giveaway dinner, then it is called a memorial. And after the memorial then you are eligible to dance. And back home, we have what is called a Sun Dance. You have probably heard about the Sun Dance, back around Fort Hill, Wyoming. It is a different type of dance. And it is what they call a dance of thirst. It is an eating dance. When you dance one dance, you owe another dance. Say my father went there last year and danced, and he died. Then the oldest son would have to dance for him. Because he owed a dance. So my older brother, Buster, he would have to dance for my father. If he wasn't able to, I would have to dance. They still do that at the formal reservations. They Sun Dance every year. They usually have two Sun Dances a year at Fort Hill."

HORACE AXTELL: "Ever since I grew up, since I was a little boy, I always called it a sweathouse. There is a name for that. The word for it is *wish-de-tomo*. Our way, the sweat is not like a ceremony. Other tribes it is different. They have their own ways. I still tell my young people, 'We have our ways too.' And a lot of these people are going out and maybe think it is neat to sing songs in a sweathouse or pray or do all these other things. But as long as I remember, we never did these things. It wasn't a ceremony. We have our religion, a longhouse, the place to go worship. That is one category of spirituality. And then we have games, playing games, like stick game. And then we have war games. We have serenades. We have a sweathouse all separate. We don't combine all together like a lot of tribes do. So that is what I tell my young people. We don't have to go out and do things the other tribes do. Maybe these guys might think it is neat. That may be. But we are Nez Percé. Our people didn't do things that way. So the sweathouses that I remember, [that's] still the way I do it.

"The sweathouse . . . we called him the Old Man. Nez Percé call him the *tewe*. It means Old Man. He is like a medicine man. He is like a healer. He has got wisdom. And he has got all the knowledge of the old ways. So when we go in there, we talk to this Old Man. We don't talk to the creator. That is somebody else. That is different. We don't use them kind of prayers. We don't even pray. We just talk to him. Thank him for allowing us to clean our body. Strengthen our souls. And the medicine that he has in the rocks and water . . . so it is a little different. And it is ordinary. It is not a ceremony.

"But still our young people are going out and doing these things. And they go out to the Sun Dances. And they are doing a lot of other things that other tribes do. But I tell them, 'Well, if you are going to do that, you do it good. We don't want to be bringing stuff home and using it when we really don't know what it means.' Of course, at least we know what our traditions and culture mean. That is the way I put it across. I have seen guys come to our sweathouse with a broken heart. Like the man who lost his wife. She died. Very lonely. Told him to sweat with us for a whole week. And he got healed. Never did sing songs or anything. Or pray in there. Just come to the Old Man and ask for help. First three or four times he went to the sweathouse, he just quiet. He wouldn't say anything. He would come out and sit by himself out there. Go back in. But the last two days, he start beginning to talk. Beginning to laugh. Began to tell stories inside the sweat lodge. The Old Man helped him.

"That is the kind of things that I have seen in my life. And I guess that is maybe so different to the young people now. But I teach my sons the way I do it. That is one of the things that I know is our way. And each family had their own place. Their own sweathouse. And it was always welcome. So when we left someplace, or go and have a sweat, and tell the Old Man we are going to leave for a while. So he was there taking care of the whole house, everything. But when we come back, we would go to the Old Man [thanking him] for taking care of everything while I was gone. That is how important he was. He still is.

"And then we have another, similar to the sweat. But it is called the mud bath. It is more of a healing, like for arthritis, or skin disease. I was told that the old people used to prepare themselves for war this way. Make themselves strong. They use a little bit bigger rocks. And they heat them the same way. Only they filled it right close to the creek. Dig a hole about the size of a sweathouse. And they run this water into the hole. So they can sit down in there in the water and have the water this deep. And the water gets muddy. They heat these rocks, and you have a pit that you dug. Then you dig a little deeper hole for the rocks to fall into. Push them all into that one side. And then you sit in there, and the water gets pretty hot. And you sit in there just like a hot spring. And come out and wash off like you do at the sweathouse. Only thing is you do this early in the morning, just about daybreak. I hear guys talk about that now. Yeah. I used to go mud bath. We used to do it for a whole week. And I just kind of shake my head because a man can't stand it for a whole week. Three days, you are drained out pretty good. It makes you weak. But then you can rebuild your strength really fast. You are unafraid. Your courage is built up. And there is a name for that too. They call it *to-may-an-wess.* All this Mother Earth cures you. You are getting from Mother Earth all this healing. Cleansing. And I have done that."

MYLIE LAWYER: "My father said that a long time ago they would make lean-tos out of branches and shrubs. Gradually they use the tules from the edge of the water. They pull those out and dry them. And then they lace them together with sinew. And maybe they'll make them about six or seven feet long. And then they put them around the poles to make a tule tepee. My dad said my first home was a tule tepee. And I said, 'Did it leak?' And he said, 'No. If it rained or snowed, those reeds would swell up and it would be waterproof.'"

PAT COURTENAY GOLD: "The other thing characteristic of the Wasco people were bowls that they carved. Wooden bowls. And we also steamed sheep horn to use as spoons. And then not only did we shape them and steam them for the spoons, but we also carved them. And all of those skills were lost. The basketry was also lost. When I grew up I didn't know any Wasco Indian who wove baskets. And my family didn't even have the traditional Wasco baskets. I only saw them in museums. We did have the Klickitat baskets."

MYLIE LAWYER: "We have Chief Lawyer's spoon. It is made out of mountain sheep horn. And we have his wife's. It is a smaller one. And we have Chief Timothy's that is a little bit smaller than Chief Lawyer's. But they are made out of the horn of an animal. And I asked Dad, 'How did they do it?' And he said his grandmother told him that they boil it. They boil the horn until it is soft. And then they cut it and shape it. And we have those. We have three spoons. They made bowls out of wood. This Tony Earl that lives down below us, come up on some that were so high like this. And they were burnt out in the center. And those were used for cooking. And then they had baskets. And they put the hot rocks in them to cook if they were going to cook."

HORACE AXTELL: "Well, the thing, I think, in my boyhood, was the love of horses. I used to ride a horse every day. My grandmother had some horses. And we used to use them for pulling the wagon. And done a lot of things with a wagon and a horse. Haul wood. Haul a lot of stuff. Plow the field. Took a long time to work with horses. And travel with horses."

ED EDMO: "I used to hunt up in the Yakima reservations. And my grandfather was Yakima. He worked as a guard at the Yakima Guard Station at the reservation. When he was in the summertime working up there, I used to stay with them in the summertime. I used to be able to hunt with them. We would go up there and hunt in the evenings. It was a lot of fun. We used to go up there, mostly for deer and elk. Just before fall we would get an elk. But deer, we mostly hunt deer. And I think I was thirteen years old when I shot my first deer. I was thirteen, and my grandfather gave me the gun that I shot it with. A .32 Winchester Special. I had that for years. Got lever action. Looked like a .30–30. Same kind of frame."

MYLIE LAWYER: "Are you familiar with the *parfleche*? Well, that is what they used. My dad said that his grandmother kept one for dry meat. It had grease on it and everything. And she would wipe it out and clean it, and put it in the sun and get it ready because they were going to go hunting. Because she would dry the meat up there and pack it very carefully because you had to keep it good because it has got to last you all winter. That is what they ate. And then they had the boxes. And I can remember my South Dakota grandmother having these boxes of the rawhide with the painted stuff on them under her bed. One for socks, and one for underwear, and one for different things. And on the other side for her husband. Because they didn't have bureau drawers, or they didn't have anything. And that is what they used. And my brother and I looked in books and everything about how you dry meat.

"I lived one whole summer down to Celilo because we had to take census. They were trying to decide what they were going to do with Celilo. Whether it would go to Warm Springs or Yakima or Umatilla, or whoever. So I counted Indians that come there. And I knew how many come from the Nez Percé and how many come from every tribe. And I kept track that whole summer. And I thought, 'Well, I am going to learn from these women.' And I learned how to clean a salmon, and cut it up. And you get it out so far. And you put sticks in it. Then put it on the racks.

"So my brother and I thought, well, we are going to do it, because we own land up there where we could kill deer—every night we would see the deer. So we did it. I got a tepee from Crow. And it turned out good. And then they made a pemmican. And these Indians did it too. They pounded up their meat with their mortar and pestle. Pounded it real fine. And then they put either huckleberries or dried chokecherries, or the dried Juneberries. They call it serviceberries. Any kind of dried berries that had a little sweetening to it. And then they used the fat from the animal that generally is around the kidneys. They would render it out and they would mix it in while it was melted. And then they either made cakes out of it, or they just kept it loose. And if they were going to travel, they made cakes about the size of a hamburger. And then they would just take their flint knife and cut it off and they would eat it. And it is good. So my South Dakota grandmother introduced us to that. And we just thought it was just wonderful. We are going to make some. And they used the back strip right under the spine. It is part of a rib steak. Rib eye.

"So he went out and killed three deer. And it took us time to get it ready and everything. So I cut it. And we dried them three days and three nights. He took care of the nights and I took care of the day. And we pounded it up real good. His wife helped us. We went to the slaughterhouse and I got the fat that I wanted and rendered it out and strained it and fixed it. And we put the dried currants from the grocery store in. . . . And little sugar. And we ate it up in one night. All that work. But he said, 'Shall I go get three more?' We had fun doing that."

ALLEN PINKHAM: "In the beginning, we didn't have to go through court to win back hunting and fishing rights, which we had been doing since the late 1950s to the present. But now it has gone into other issues like gathering and grazing. Because gathering, we used to dig roots, camas roots, caus roots, and other medicinal herbs out in the mountains where these forestlands are now. And so now it is because the impacts upon the resources, the habitats, and the water quality, and those kinds of things. I am very concerned about the conservation ethic of some of these resources. We need to make sure that we take care of these resources. And they are on public lands. The Forest Service doesn't know a lot of these resources that we utilize. They probably know about the major ones like camas and caus, and cedar bark and some of those things. But overall I think they need to understand that there are other resources that we utilize from these lands."

Oral tradition is the foundation of cultural preservation. Not only does it include myths that hold in place cultural intuitive ties to homeland and lore about hunting, gathering, food preparation, and myriad other survival skills; it also provides historical perspective that doesn't necessarily coincide with that of the professional historian or extra-cultural documentarian. Mylie Lawyer recalls the circumstances when her great-grandfather was the first of the Nez Percé people to actually observe the coming of the Lewis and Clark expedition to the Nez Percé homeland in 1805.

MYLIE LAWYER: "Great-grandfather Twisted Hair was up at Wee-Ike with the Indians. They were digging camas. He was a little boy about nine or ten years old.

And he was the first one that saw the Lewis and Clark expedition. He and his two companions. They were named Wachamu and Tiklo Naciscan. And they said, 'What do we do?' They first saw buffalo. 'Well, we got no buffalo in this country.' And they sneaked up through the bushes, and they saw these people with a lot of hair on their faces. So he said, 'We better go back.'

"So they ran back to Twisted Hair's tepee. And they told him. And Twisted Hair sent them around to the different camps. 'You go over there to Red Bear. You go over there to the different camps and tell them to come because we have got to have a meeting quick.' And the chiefs come. And they decided, 'What do we do? Should we kill them?' They said, 'Yeah. Let's kill them. And we will throw them in the river.' These little boys, three of them, were watching, and they listened to all of them. And Great-grandfather Lawyer told his wife, 'We laid on our bellies.' In the hot weather they roll up their tepees. He said, 'We laid on our bellies and listened to them talk about what they were going to do.' So they decided that they would be ready for them. And of course, when they saw Lewis come up with ribbons, you know, he thought that they would be crazy about . . . but he [Great-grandfather] is the first one that saw Lewis and Clark."

Many Indian people on the North American continent have strongly resisted being spiritually and intellectually subsumed by the dominant culture and its governing bodies. Many have expressed that they perceive the collective attitude inherent in Western culture as biased mainly by science, technology, politics, and a system of economics intent on turning habitat into money, regardless of the consequences. Virtually all Indian cultures have been guided primarily by the spirit of Nature. While some Indian people have embraced variations of the Christian religion introduced to the Western Hemisphere in 1492, many more have retained the spiritual attitudes that have sustained them for thousands of years. In this way, they perpetuate the spirit of place.

Indian people have lived within the watershed of the Columbia and Snake river system for at least 12,000 years. Over the last century, they have seen their homeland and waterways invaded by timber, agricultural, and mining industries, the construction of a series of dams, and the presence of the Hanford facility, which discharges nuclear waste into the river. Many Indians fail to understand the mentality of a culture that seems oblivious to such acts of abuse against the environment. Instead, the Earth is seen by traditional indigenous peoples as a living organism that gave birth to all species. People who live close to the flow of Nature know intuitively that wanton destruction of habitat and thoughtless introduction of toxic materials weakens the health of the ecosystem upon which we all rely.

Many Indians, including Nez Percé Allen and Jamie Pinkham, are well educated within the milieu of Western culture, but their perspective is of much broader scope than is generally found among most modern Americans.

ALLEN PINKHAM: "There is sunlight. There is earth, and water. Three basic elements. Without those three elements you would not have life at all. See, when the sunlight comes and it touches Mother Earth, the mineral soil, it needs water. And when you add water to that, sunlight, earth, water . . . that is the creation of life. And all the species are connected to that. So if it wasn't for sunlight, we wouldn't have life. If it wasn't for Mother Earth, we wouldn't have life. And if it wasn't for water we wouldn't have life. East is significant for us. When the sun rises in the morning, it gives us the light for that day. And then it goes to the heavens and goes around. And it is nighttime. My dad always used to complain: 'Oh, these non-Indians always say that we are worshipping the sun.' Well we are. Because it gives us life and strength. But we also realize that the sun was placed in that position by our creator. We honor the sun for what it provides. Everything is connected to those three elements."

JAMIE PINKHAM: "The way that I was taught was that we were the last, therefore the youngest, creatures put on this Earth. And I think even our creation legend reflects that. And while at birth we were given some abilities and some knowledge, we don't have all the strength and knowledge to survive in this world. And so who do we always turn to, to learn these skills, to gain this knowledge to survive? We turn to our elders. And our elders are those older living beings, like the plants and animals, who were here long before us. And so I think that creates dependency upon nature then that is different. Spiritual and physical dependency. We also look to Nature, those lessons of everyday life. Community, courage, passion, devotion. When you look at the livelihood of animals, and when you draw from their examples, it teaches us something about life. I think the way that we look at the environment is, we don't look at it for its economic properties. We have always understood that we didn't have dominion over Nature. We weren't out to conquer Nature, because Nature was our caretaker, our provider. And my personal view is to dispel this notion that the American Indian was a natural resource manager long before the coming of the Europeans. We did not manage Nature. We didn't make the salmon run. We didn't make the berries, the foods, the medicines grow, actually because we responded to Nature, to the change in seasons. So actually, I feel that Nature managed us. Because we put our welfare into the hands of our creator. And into the hands of Nature. Our caregiver. So I always feel that it has always been the other way around. That Nature managed us, and provided for our livelihood.

"I think that the greatest jeopardy that we see as far as the natural habitat is our rivers. Our water. The pressures that the development of the West has placed upon the waterways, the dams for power generation, for irrigation to provide for barge traffic, those types of things. We look at the headwaters. The impacts of mining, logging, and grazing have put tremendous burdens upon our stream systems. Salmon to the Nez Percé was like the buffalo to the plains. You change the water, you change the salmon. When you change the salmon, you change the Nez Percé people. I think our river systems are those things that we need to focus our strongest attention to. Before we can truly heal the land, we need to care for ourselves and for one another. Because it was the feeling that as we learn to abuse ourselves and one another, we lost sight of living within Nature's limits, because we wanted to gain more than we dare leave behind. And with that mentality, I think we start pushing ourselves into this kind of spiritual bankruptcy. And with that we lost sight of our moral obligation to Nature. And so we see our rivers being dammed up. We see pesticides being put onto the land, which pollutes the aquifer and gets into our river systems. We see a storage of nuclear waste adjacent to river systems. And there needs to be almost a refocus. A refocus in our relationship with each other as human beings. And once we create that healthy relationship, then I think we can begin to do a better job of focusing how we heal the environment.

"We see so much fractionalization in this country, with the different interests. Freedom has been a great thing for this country. But in essence, freedom has left us a little bit vulnerable. Freedom has allowed this country to be built on a variety of heritages. The mining heritage. The farming heritage. The timber heritage. But also we have religious and ethnic heritages, including Indian people. And freedom has allowed that to happen. But the vulnerability of that is that with this, some heritages have been built at the expense of another. Some are held more politically sacred. So we have these conflicts that arise, and this division within our communities. The thing to focus on is that we are blessed with many heritages, but we only have one Mother Earth, and that is the Earth upon which we prove ourselves to our creator. And so we need to reconcile these human differences that exist between us. And once we start reconciling those differences, then I truly think that we become cohesive enough to really make a deliberate and sincere effort to restore the natural ecosystem that not just the Nez Percé depend on but really all of this country depends on."

ALLEN PINKHAM: "I know a little bit about Hanford. They do discharge acceptable levels of radiation into the Columbia River system. Is this acceptable level of radiation really acceptable? It is maybe acceptable for this generation of people that utilize resources out of the Columbia River. But what about succeeding generations? I think we are trying to cover it up by saying it doesn't exist when we bury it. It is just saying, 'Let's not contend with this problem right now.' We should contend with this problem right now. Like any other resource, we need to be involved with the restoration, protection of resources right now, rather than pass it on to the next generation to worry about it. Why don't we accept a little bit of pain right now, so that five or six generations down the line, they don't have to suffer pain a hundred times of what we have to suffer now?

"We are a comfort-seeking species. There is an ecosystem of sustainable resources that have got to be protected and enhanced for the benefit of all mankind. Nuclear waste is a major issue. Bury it, get it out of sight, and it will go away. It is not going to go away. Half-life of nuclear waste is 10,000 years. So all we are doing is passing that problem on to some generation thousands of years down the road for some catastrophic event to occur that will expose people to radiation, or it will seep into the aquifer.

"There is a lot of farming. Herbicides, insecticides, fertilizers . . . go into the Columbia River system. And we eat the salmon that comes out of the Columbia River system. So it is affecting us. It may not affect me because I don't look sick right now. But I eat that salmon. And I don't know what it is doing to me. It may not affect me in my lifetime. But it may affect grandchildren or great-grandchildren. They say acceptable levels, because we don't turn sick right now. We got to think further ahead than just a five-year plan. Most businesses and corporations and organizations say, 'Well, let's deal with a five-year plan.' Why don't we develop that into 150-year plan? Plus. Many generations from us. Seven generations from what we are doing right now. Why don't we plan for that seventh generation? Because that is the one that is going to accept everything that we do today. That generation will be the most affected. And nobody can think that far ahead, because the corporate way of thinking today is only five years, maybe ten or fifteen.

"We can't discount totally the value of Western science and technology. We have this wisdom that goes way back. And what we need to do is combine this wisdom with this newfound science and technology to guide the care of our land and our communities. We need to do a better job of combining those two together. One should not be displaced or pushed aside at the expense of another."

The Indian village of Celilo was a major trading center for many thousands of years. Peoples from myriad tribes traditionally gathered there to fish at Celilo Falls and to trade and socialize. It was there that alliances were sealed, marriages were arranged, and traditional gambling was practiced. Celilo Falls was a geophysical site that was woven into many legends and provided the mythic parameters that held Indian cultures in place. Such was the strength of Celilo Falls.

The present-day older generation of Native Americans in the greater watershed of the Columbia River was the last to frequent Celilo Falls, this traditional center for salmon fishing that was intertribally held in common by indigenous peoples for at least 12,000 years. On March 10, 1957, Celilo Falls was inundated when the United States Army Corps of Engineers closed the floodgates on their newly constructed dam, thus flooding this ancient site, which resulted in cultural impoverishment for thousands of Indian peoples whose hundreds of generations of ancestors had honored this sacred place. The flooding of Celilo Falls was regarded by some as an act of techno-fantastic madness, by others as yet one more act of infamy committed by the prevailing government, and by everyone as a consummate tragedy.

MYLIE LAWYER: "I think Celilo was one of the greatest trading points for this whole northwest because they traded everything. And did you know that some Nez Percé traded and got a Klamath woman? They traded people because a lot of them gambled. And they just gambled everything, and they had horse races. It must have been a really crowded place. This old lady that I talked to said that her grandmother told them that it was so crowded sometimes that you didn't have any place to put your fish. A lot of times people went there for the purpose of trading if they had something and they wanted something. That was a purpose of the Nez Percé being a transitional people. They could bring down buffalo hides from the plains. And they could bring white turnips. They had dried buffalo meat that anybody would just give anything for. And they traded for generations and generations. Even from northern California, people come up there to trade. And that is where they learned about horses. The Nez Percé, when they heard about it, before they had horses, they sent four men down there to look for horses. And they got them and brought them back."

ED EDMO: "Celilo was a great gathering place. I remember when I was a youngster in my teens, there were all types of tribes from Montana, Idaho, Oregon, Washington. Even some from clear down south as Klamath Falls, all came to fish there. And it was a place where they made a living. The main culture was Yakima and Warm Springs, the most dominant tribes here. You know Indian people, they don't mind intermarriages. Like my father married a Nez Percé. So that is how he got to be here."

PAT COURTENAY GOLD: "When we used to go fishing, we used to go down to Celilo Falls, and that was another really nice experience. I am beginning to understand why we have a lot of social problems on the reservation. A lot of our legends and valued beliefs with the Wasco and the Warm Springs people, who also came from farther upriver . . . we lost a lot of our culture when we moved to the reservation. I was about five or six years old when we used to always travel down to the river during the spring and the fall [salmon] runs. All of our family was down and everybody was fishing. And this was just before most of the dams were built, and we still had good salmon runs. My mother took me and my oldest sister, and it was a really hot day. The falls, we would have all of these falls, and then they would come down on all this basalt rock. The spray. It just creates this huge spray. And it was always nice to go down there because of this spray.

"It was really hot and dry. Hardly had any humidity. And you go down to the falls, and there is all this humidity from the spray. Well, my mother always took us down, but she never took us from on top down to where the falls were. Well, this time, she decided to take me and my sister down. This is all basalt rock. So the fisherman had put planks of wood down. And you had to be careful, because when the mist came up and got the planks wet, it could be slippery. So my mother took us partway down. As we got closer to the falls, the roar of the falls was so loud that she told us that she didn't want to take us any farther because we wouldn't be able to hear her talk. So she said, 'You stay here and wait until I come back. Don't move. Just stay here.' So she had us hold hands so we would stay there. And my mother walked away from the falls. And I think she went no more than six feet away, and she disappeared in the mist. That is how close we were to the falls, and the mist. Later she told us that when she went down there, she would have to talk in sign language. They also had a sign language to bargain. And she had got directions to where her relatives were fishing. So she would go down in the mist. And half the time she would see these misty figures. She would stop them and ask them in sign language where so-and-so's scaffold was so she could go and get salmon there.

"When my sister and I were standing waiting, as the wind shifted, the mist would also shift. And it would cover us and then go away and then cover us. And we loved that sensation. But what I really remember visually from the falls, you were just like in a different world. You didn't know up from down. Left from right. And the sun was shining and the mist was going. And as the mist was moving, there would be these little circled rainbows. They were just dancing around. And as this sunshine moved and the mist moved, then they would either disappear or they would move. And I remember that so vividly. It was such a neat experience."

ED EDMO: "My dad came here in 1939. And he was walking down The Dalles on 2nd Street where the chamber of commerce was. He said he saw a picture of The Dalles Dam. And he went and told the elders of Celilo that they were going to build a dam out here. He saw the drawings. And they said, no, it would never happen because we were under this treaty. But he says, 'It's the way it goes. It looks like they got the OK of the government.' And sure enough it happened. That was way back in '39 or '38 or something when my dad saw that. My dad talked about that quite a bit."

PAT COURTENAY GOLD: "It was a real hardship for them to move. We were up around The Dalles area, right around Celilo Falls. And we were sort of the key people that did the trading with all of the tribes that came up and down the Columbia River. The Columbia and the tributaries were like freeways and highways. And they all met in that area. One of the reasons the Wascos were a key trading tribe was because of all the fish. The salmon. And after, literally, tons and tons of salmon were harvested, that location was really crucial for drying and preparing the salmon. There were these really dry east winds that came down the river. So you could catch a lot of fish down around the mouth of the Columbia River. But you didn't have the dry winds to really preserve the fish. So after we caught all the salmon then we dried the salmon, and then we would pound it into a powder. So you would get this huge thirty- to fifty-pound salmon, dry it, which you dehydrate it. Then you get maybe half its weight. And when you got the dried meat from the salmon, then you would pound that. So you would get this huge salmon and it would fill up a little basket. Just a little eight-inch basket, six inches in diameter, eight inches high. And that is what we traded. So the Wasco people were well known for the trade that they did. And that is where our tradition of weaving the baskets came from because we are constantly trading not only the salmon, but the salmon was stored in the baskets. And we were trading the baskets and the salmon together. So at that time there was no way that we could lose the skill of weaving the baskets. You just had to make them all the time. So historically we were a trading people. And we were well known for our baskets because we had those geometric designs that were real characteristic of the Wasco people. And after the treaties were signed, and we were moved, we were moved southward about a hundred miles to the Warm Springs reservation. So that move was really traumatic, culturally, to our tribe. Our history, our culture, our legends were all based on the Columbia River. And it was our Wasco stories tied in with the Columbia River. After we moved we still had the right to go back to the river to fish. We also had the right to go out and dig roots and get different fibers for whatever uses we want. Primarily for basket-making. But when we were moved, the next step was to Christianize the Indians and to put them in boarding schools, the theory being to break the Indian culture and to make white people out of Indians. And it just didn't work. There are really sad stories about the breakup of the families and the ties, and the loss of the traditional skills that they had."

ED EDMO: "It was sad you know, because the year that we moved in '56, we moved to Wishram. I don't know if it was June or July. We all went to Celilo and burned houses. They told us to burn them down. So we went down there. And we burned our house, our grandmother's house, my uncle's house, my other uncle's house. My auntie's house. We burned our own homes. And that was kind of sad, just something you never see again. And I remember, I skipped school that day they opened the dam. The day they opened it, I skipped school and went to the mission and watched the Celilo get flooded. And I watched it get higher and higher and higher. And I remember watching that thing. And boy, I can't believe it. It just kept getting filled up. Old folks watching. I went by myself. I went down to the Train Bridge. And I imagine I was crying. It was a real hard thing. It has never been the same since. The younger people got mixed emotions, and all that stuff. But pretty hard to say what it is like. For me, you can't live in the past. So I just went in the military and kicked around for a while. Goofed off for a while. Then finally settled down and went to work."

PAT COURTENAY GOLD: "People in the basket world, collectors and those who are familiar with the local native cultures, are fascinated with the baskets and the designs. And I would say the majority are uncomfortable when I do variations of the designs. And my variations include putting modern dresses on the traditional geometric figures. And I like to experiment with colors. So I put bright colors on them. I will weave beads in too, to dress them up. And then the other thing that I do, I am concerned about the health of the river. On the Columbia River we have this great big place called Hanford which did a lot research in uranium and plutonium, never really considering the side effect of what this is going to do to the land. Well, there is a big controversy over the radioactivity in the Columbia River. And the people in the nuclear industry claimed that it is there. But it is something that we don't have to worry about since it is such small amounts. Those who know a lot about radioactive decay, and realize that there is the thing called half-life, that there is no way that you are ever going to completely get rid of it. Because we are never told exactly whether it is uranium or plutonium, or whether it is radioactive iodine. And just what is it? And what is the whole synergistic effect of all these radioactive products? But those of use who live along the river have seen maimed and deformed salmon. Maimed and deformed sturgeon. And we know that there is a long-term effect. And if it is just now showing up, what is it going to be like in the next generations?

"So, getting back to my baskets, I do a lot of the traditional salmon images. And one of the Wasco images that reflects strength and longevity is the sturgeon. And the sturgeon do get huge. They get to be over six feet. There are some of them that have been caught. And they are eight feet. And they are big. And then they live a long life. So what I do in my designs is always put deformed sturgeon on my designs. And now people who know me really well come up to me and say, 'Where is your Hanford sturgeon?' So that is why I call it the Hanford sturgeon."

JAMIE PINKHAM: "As Indian people, because of our relationship with the land, when we become an advocate for the land, for healthy environment, we are an advocate for everyone across this land. Because the American Indian is a minority population, a minority landowner within our own homeland, we are still seen as a mystery, as an unknown. If we can break past some of the barriers that have either displaced or dismissed the wisdom or the abilities, the talents of Indian people, I think we can start reaching out to a broader community. You listen to this world. And it is calling for cultural diversity. And to me it is a cry for help. Because I think in order for us to survive and be prosperous, we need to bring in all the diverse ideals and values that have survived the test of time. For Indian people have survived in the face of adversity over all these years. But there are lessons. There are teachings there. And I think if we can help people understand our point of view, get past these old barriers that scare people away—about Indian sovereignty, Indian treaty rights—and get rid of some of those misperceptions, get through the smoke, the mirrors, and the clouds that are out there and truly start interacting, helping people understand where our values are rooted and what our values mean. I think everybody is willing to accept a healthy environment. But at times I think we always put the science, the technology in front in our debates. And we need to put the spiritual part right up there too. The debates about the environment have gone well beyond the scientific and technological debates, and as Al Gore said, they now include moral debates. And I think we need to get people to begin to feel within their heart the passion and devotion that it is going to take to change the world and the way we look at the world. And not do it with just science and politics or technology and economics but really to get back the human moral side of a healthy environment."

Many Indian people have retained the perspectives of their forebears, a perspective founded in what poet and philosopher Gary Snyder calls the "practice of the wild." Many remain attuned to the respective habitats, and possess an intuitive and practical knowledge accumulated over countless generations of experience. For them, cultural diversity and biotic diversity are interlocked. This is true of indigenous cultures throughout the world. The eminent biologist Edward O. Wilson uttered a truth appropriate for all native peoples when he wrote [in *The Future of Life*]:

Unfortunately much of the indigenous knowledge is being lost as European culture continues to intrude. As the last preliterate native cultures in native countries weaken and disappear, we are losing irretrievably, what is in a real sense, scientific knowledge.

ii.

European contact gradually shattered the fabric of almost every native culture in the golden landscape of what is now called California. The Native Americans whose lands were seized in the names of kings and an alien God were forced to adapt or perish. Through the extraordinary strength of character and perseverance of groups of gifted Native American culture bearers, many tribes survived, if not in tact, at least in spirit. One of the great universal symbols of cultural continuity and integrity is the art of basket weaving—a demanding craft that requires discipline, presence of mind, talent and skill, and an evolved sense of aesthetics. Sarah Greensfelder recognized the power of basket weaving as a force for re-strengthening commitment to Native American traditions and cultural practices. She, and a small group of Native American women, formed the California Indian Basketweavers Association in 1992. Since then CIBA, as their organization is known, has involved hundreds of Indian basket weavers in California and has influenced many more throughout the nation and beyond.

In 1996, I had the opportunity to interview several members of CIBA. They are Kathy Wallace of Karok and Yurok descent, and a member of the Hoopa tribe; Dee Dominguez of Chumash descent; Jennifer Bates, a northern Miwok from the Tuolumne Rancheria; and Cassandra Hensher, a Native American of Karok descent. Sarah Greensfelder is an Anglo born into a bohemian family, and lives in the Sierra Nevada of central California.

SARAH GREENSFELDER: "My stated purpose is to preserve, promote, and perpetuate the indigenous basketry traditions of California. I would say that the real purpose is to make sure that there is a living, healthy, vibrant tradition that can be passed on to future generations. I think that the people who are part of CIBA, the women and the men, are doing a wonderful job of that. I believe that the primary motivation for doing this work for most of our members is not so that they can make baskets to sell, but to preserve a great tradition and cultural heritage, a tribal identity that brings them a great deal of closeness to the Earth. And also creates wonderful works of art and utilitarian objects that are still used today."

KATHY WALLACE: "Basket weaving was used in every aspect of our lives. It was just always there from the time a baby was born, carried in a baby basket. Later on we made baby rattles. It [the basket] was used for all the food gathering and processing, trapping animals, storing things, carrying things, all the way through to the different ceremonies. There were lots of ceremonies. There are certain baskets that are used just only in a specific ceremony, made just specifically for that. And then even all the way into death when our people fed the dead for three days after they died. And it is with a brand-new basket. Someone will make a very simple unadorned basket just for that purpose."

DEE DOMINGUEZ: "When I am weaving, it is like I am somewhere else. When I weave, I can't carry on a conversation. I cannot watch a TV program. I cannot listen. I am just looking at the plants that are in my hands. For me, my heart sings when I weave. I am not saying a word, but my heart is singing. And sometimes I don't even understand what it is saying. But it is singing. And its emotions are just going through your hands. And you are praying to your basket because you want it to be the best basket there is. Just like, I guess it would be like when a woman is pregnant, and you are talking to your child before it is born. And you know that it is going to be beautiful. And you really love it. And you are taking care of yourself as best you can so that that child will be so healthy and beautiful. And you give it everything you can. The same thing is with your basket."

JENNIFER BATES: "You know the big burden baskets used for gathering acorn and berries, and what have you. We have our winnowers. When you are doing your acorn, there is one process where you have your dried acorn. But the acorns have a red skin on it like a peanut does. And you have to take that red skin off. Some people say the red skin adds to the bitterness. But a lot of the elders told me that if you made acorn, and you had a lot of that red in your acorn, you would get talked about as being a bad cook. You just were not a good cook. And so I make sure that all of my red is out of my acorn. But anyhow, the winnower would be used in the old days too, to put your dried acorns in that. And then you would throw it up, and you would toss the acorns up in the air, and you would catch it back in that basket. And the red skin flies off. That is one way to help clean it. So there are your winnowing baskets. And you had your picking baskets. Or like berry baskets that you just individually put it around your shoulder and put things in there. And then you can just throw it into the burden basket, which is a big cone-shaped one that carries a lot of whatever you are gathering. And the men made a lot of baskets that dealt with traps. Hunting-type things. We had bird traps and fish traps. And they also made the big burden baskets for gathering such. And then you had your cooking baskets. Your storage baskets. Seed beaters. Again that is for when you are out there collecting elderberries, or different seeds that were used for salt or what have you. Mostly everything was utilitarian in the old days. And then later on you started getting the gift baskets. They also had gift baskets in the old days. They were things that were used for ceremonial purposes. Holding rattles, or medicines and things like that. Sometimes they were very small. And sometimes they were boat-shaped. And they held on to objects that were used for medicine and doctoring. I think that pretty much covers the different kinds of baskets that you would find in a home."

CASSANDRA HENSHER: "It seems to me like there are a lot of tools that are used when you are gathering. Of course you need something sharp to cut sticks or to cut the roots. Like we use clippers for cutting these days, and knives for scraping the bark off the root. The willow sticks you can just peel with your hand, and your teeth. A lot of things go into your mouth when you are doing this work. When we are doing twining, we also use an awl. But we use it in a very different way than coilers use it. Coiling basket weavers use an awl kind of like a needle. They poke a hole where they can then put the piece of root that is kind of like a thread where they poke a hole in the basket, so they can put that through there. And we use an awl just to pull the stitches down. I don't know what they call it when you are weaving on a loom. But you have those forks to pull the yarn tighter together. That is kind of how we use an awl. We pull the stitches down close together. When you are weaving small stuff you just can't do it with your fingers. It is too big and awkward. And then it seems like each weaver has their own tools. Something that they have customized or found in their house that they like to use. I guess the essentials for weaving are always a knife and an awl."

KATHY WALLACE: "About 80 percent of the work is in the gathering and the processing of your materials. Each material has to be gathered at a different time of the year that is very specific to that plant. When it says optimum, it is used for basketry material. And a lot of the things have to be taken care of for a long time before they get to that point. A lot of our materials have to be burned the year before, or in the case of hazel, two years before. So it is an ongoing process. It is not just go out in the field and pick things. You really have to know a lot about plants and their growth cycles, and the weather and the growing conditions in the soil, and how much water things have, to know what are good materials and what is not worth bothering. And then basket weavers today, not only if they find a good spot, the next year it may not be there. It may be grazed over, fenced off, built over, roads gone through it. It might be flooded and under a lake. So you are constantly having to look all year long. Because when you find something, you think, 'OK, I am going to come back when it is the right time,' or 'That looks like that needs to be pruned and it might be a good spot.' So it is just an ongoing thing all year long. And we start gathering in the early spring. Probably in February. And I gather all the way through about Thanksgiving."

DEE DOMINGUEZ: "In the city where I live, Covina, there is a creek there near my home that is actually in a canyon. And you can't really see that. It is not easily accessible because it is surrounded by residential area. And the streets are very zigzagged. So to go to that area, you wouldn't normally go there unless you were going somewhere there. Not just passing through. And there we have found our deer grass, juncus, sumac, willow, elderberry, California walnut for dyeing our materials. However, the growth area of those plants . . . well basically the juncus and the deer grass is very small. And the juncus provides us with some materials. And we have to go elsewhere. But the deer grass is only six plants that we just located a week ago. So what I am doing at this time is in the juncus and the deer-grass area, is we will be planting seedlings, and increasing that growth area to a point to where it would be able to accommodate the basket weavers with the juncus that they would need from that area. The same with the deer grass. The deer grass is in a very steep area. So not only are we going to introduce seedlings to increase that growth area, but also we need to find a way to make it accessible to the weavers so they can get up to it without disturbing the area very much."

JENNIFER BATES: "One of the things I have learned through all the experience of becoming a basket weaver is that you don't question your elders when they tell you how to do something. I remember we once went out to go collect redbud, which is what we use for design. And we both thought that we were just doing a hell of a good job. We were just splitting that material, and we cleaned it up and everything. And we had gotten a couple of rolls of redbud. And so we took it to one of our basket-weaver friends in Northport to show her what we did, because she had told us when to go get it, and, we thought, how to split it. And I guess we weren't listening. Because we went back and we showed her what we did. And she said, 'This is not good.' And I go, 'What do you mean it is no good?' And she goes, 'It is not good. You split it wrong.' And we found out that day that you have to split those nodes in half. And we were just splitting. Just splitting because we thought we were so good at splitting. And that was an accomplishment. And I went, 'She doesn't know what she is talking about.' So I took that material home and I used it. And sure enough, like she told me, if you were to use that material and put it through your basket, that if you didn't split it right on those nodes, it gets stuck on your stitch, and it just splits, or it takes off the bark. And sure enough, all those bundles that we did were bad. And we had to throw them away. And from that day on I said, 'I will never question an elder or anybody who teaches me something. Because they know.' And sometimes you want to question that. You want to go, 'Well, how do you know that?' And then you also want to put in new technology. And well, we did it this way. And it won't work. What if we went and gathered it now because of this and this and this? And you are going, 'It won't work.' From that day forward I knew that if anybody said anything about when you gather and how you gather, that is how it is. That is how it has been handed down. You don't change it. And that was a lesson to be learned there for me, and that was a big one because we had gotten so much redbud. And I felt bad that we wasted it all. And I was mad at myself for not even understanding that you listen to the people who know what they are doing."

Cassandra Hensher: "In our area, a watertight basket needs a conifer root. We use the spruce root because we get it there on the coast. And that kind of root will swell up when it is wet. And of course you weave it as tight as you can. And then when you put the water in it, the roots swell, and they hold the water in. Just works. And that is used for a lot of stuff. For cooking baskets, for eating bowls. Water dippers. Cooking baskets are rather large bowls. You put some acorn flour and some water in. And at that point it is cold. And you take rocks that have been heated in the fire until they are red-hot. You put them in the basket. And in our area we stir it with a paddle. It looks like a little oar, like a miniature boat paddle. And you stir the rocks. If you don't stir them, they are so hot that they will burn through the basket. It is a shame to burn a good basket. So you be real careful. You stir the rocks. It takes a little while for a big bowl. But after a while it starts to boil. And it thickens up, just like when you cook it on the stove. It boils and gets thicker. And you keep on going until it is the way you like it."

JENNIFER BATES: "When we are finished making our acorn we call it *nupa*. It is a soup. We can also make a *ulé*, which is what we call our bread. And actually what you are doing is you are making your soup very, very thick. Then you take a dipper basket and you take your thick nupa that you had, and you put that in another basket that is running cold water going through it. And in the old days you would have another basket in the water source. And you take the little dipper basket and you shake. And you just keep shaking it. And eventually the cold water gels the acorn in there. And it falls off the basket. And it kind of looks like a turnover. And that is what we call our bread. And you can slice it. And it is a Jell-O-type consistency. It just gets really thick. And it just gels up."

KATHY WALLACE: "When they do the Jump Dance ceremony, there are special baskets just for that. The women make them, give them to the men. The men finish them up, and the women never touch them again. I recently was asked to replace an old basket that was used in our ceremony up on the Klamath. I had never ever seen it before. I had two people describing it to me. And neither of them are basket weavers. And so it was really hard for me to understand what it was they wanted me to do. So I asked for a picture. They went to take a picture, and it [the basket] fell apart. And I got pictures of the parts to try and figure out how to make it. But I got help from Peg Matheson, who is not even Indian. But she recognized the basket's style immediately, told me how to do it, got me started. It took me all summer and the day that I finished that basket, and I didn't know how to end it. I didn't know how to do the braid on that. She called me. Told me how to do it over the phone. And I finished it that night. And it was just amazing that that was when she called me. Every time I would run out of sticks, somebody would come up with some more. And I was down to the last one. When I was finished, I didn't have any left. It was amazing. So that will be danced this year for the first time. And I will never see it again and never touch it again until they need a new one, maybe thirty years from now."

DEE DOMINGUEZ: "I'm trying to put myself in the position to where I'll be able to weave a basket with a rattlesnake design on it. I haven't done that yet. But to do so, I need to compose myself and put myself into that position where it is possible. So I've been reviewing all of the rattlesnake baskets that I'm able to find.

"The quail is like an arbitrator. The quail is the animal that puts things back to good order. And one time a rattlesnake told some bad stories about some

Yokuts people. And Quail knew that this was not true, and those people died because of what Rattlesnake had said. And so Quail, being the arbitrator and the person putting things back right, went and he told Water Skater, which is a snake, and he is like a messenger because he travels so fast. He can travel on land and water. And so Quail told Water Skater what had happened about this bad rattlesnake. So he traveled far on land and water, and looked and told Ant, who was very strong for being such a tiny little animal. And the little ant traveled and looked for this bad rattlesnake, bit him, and killed him and ate him. So now, when we make a rattlesnake basket, the rattlesnake design is on the basket. There are quail on there. There is water skater, and there are ants on there. And so that is to tell Rattlesnake not to tell bad stories about the Yokuts people. Because Quail, Water Skater, and Ant are there to make sure that he doesn't do that."

JENNIFER BATES: "I know a lot of weavers whose spirits go into their baskets. I really can't say that I have experienced that yet. Maybe it is because I haven't made the ultimate basket of my life yet, or something. When I make my baskets, I have some things in mind. I mean, who they are going to, and what it is going to be used for. But I haven't experienced anything overcoming me. You know, going from my hands into that basket. I know when I am working on that basket I feel really good about it. But I personally can't say that I have come across that yet. A lot of women that weave, like Mabel McKay, she is gone now. She has passed away. But she was considered a doctor woman, and also a very wonderful basket weaver. And she always explained in her baskets, there was a spirit in that basket. And she only worked on a certain basket if she dreamed about it the night before. If it came to her then she would get up that day and work on that particular basket. But they were all spirit baskets. They all had different spirits or different reasons why they were being made by her. And that could have to do with, again, if you were, like she was, a medicine woman or a doctor woman, and in my area, the Miwok people, I don't know that we had people like that. Or doctors like that that were weavers. For the most part, that I understand, the doctor people were mostly male. I don't think that we had many women who were doctor women."

KATHY WALLACE: "I know that anybody who has taken classes from Mabel McKay has a real deeper, maybe more spiritual feeling. Because she was a medicine person. And when she wove baskets, they were medicine baskets. I remember her telling me about the medicine baskets she made, and how they worked. And she explained to me how they were kind of like an X-ray. The baskets she dreamed about, it was for that person. And when she doctored, she said that she would pray and dream. And she kind of got going into kind of a trance kind of thing. And that basket, that little tiny basket would grow and grow and become transparent and cover the whole body of the person she was doctoring. And she could look into that basket and see into the person, and look into their organs and everything inside of them and find out where they were sick and where they were hurting. And she said that it was kind of like an X-ray. I thought that was very interesting. She was a very unusual person. If you didn't know who she was, she seemed very unassuming. But if you were a little bit sensitive, you could pick up on that power that she had. But she never made a big deal about it. She just always seemed so very unassuming."

Jennifer Bates: "The one that my grandmother and my aunts used to always tell us was about our fingers. And it had to do with Coyote and Lizard, and both being grandfathers. And they were arguing one day, on a hot day in the sun. And Grandfather Lizard was saying, 'Well our kids are going to have hands like me, with long fingers, so they can climb rocks and hold on to things.' And Coyote laughed and said, 'Oh no they're not. They are going to have hands like me. Short paws, so they can run fast and jump.' And they went on and on with this conversation. And it got heated, and they got mad. And Coyote said, 'That's it. I am going to eat you.' And Grandfather Lizard ran. And he got in between these rocks. And Coyote hit the rocks and he fell over. And that is why today we have hands like a lizard because Grandfather Lizard survived, and Coyote got knocked out."

Cassandra Hensher: "The people lived mostly along the rivers and traveled on the rivers in their boats. And they had to do a lot of walking. They would take the ridgelines. But our sacred area called the high country is up on the mountaintops. So while the people were living on the rivers, their sacred areas were up high. So they had a definite relationships to their entire watershed."

Kathy Wallace: "I think that we are like the spotted owl. We are just representative of where we are going, and what is going to happen to everybody. We are there because we have such an intimate and close relationship with the plants, where we are actually ingesting that. We are sticking it in our mouths and under our nails, and breathing the bark and the dust. And sticking our hands through the earth up to our elbows and tasting it. Processing that. Splitting, or chewing on, when you are going to add a new element into a basket, you chew on the ends of each one that we add in. And that is a very intimate relationship that you have with the plant and the earth where it came from.

"Other people may not have that close of a relationship with things. But other people gather and eat things out of the forest. They gather mushrooms. They gather firewood. They gather berries. They fish. They hunt. And they are having this contact too.

"And the people who manage the lands haven't ever thought of this. They haven't ever considered that when they do things to the land. Also it seems to the European culture, and at least the Forest Service, is that they always think about taming Mother Nature. Man has got this power. And they are going to tame Mother Nature. And they are going to make the forest what they want it to be. Produce all this lumber. And produce dollars. And there is a monetary drive here that is driving them. And that is why the almighty dollar is why they are doing it. That is their reason for doing it. And they are going to control everything and they are going to make it. But down here at the bottom are the things they never considered because they don't consider them of any importance. And there are things like the soil. The rocks. The bogs. The bacteria. The water. It is getting to the point, not even considering lots of times, the water. Unless it is a specific source, like a lake of drinking water, they don't consider that anything else uses that water. Butterflies, or animals, or humans. And all of these things have to be considered in a forest. A forest is more than trees. A forest is full of so many other things that are animate and inanimate things. And if you think about each of those things having a soul and feeling, you are a lot more careful how you deal with them. And if you don't consider yourself as the master of all, but only a part of the whole circle, then you do what you have to do. Your little part makes up a small part of that circle. And you are dependent on everybody and every type of people, whether it is rock people, or animal people, or plant people who do their part too. And you help each other. And man was put here to take care of those things and keep them on an even keel. That is why we still do our world renewal ceremonies to balance the Earth. To make the Earth better. That is our responsibility. It is not just a duty. It is just not something we do. It is a responsibility. That is why we are here. I don't understand how people can be so shortsighted. Basically not seeing the forest for the trees."

iii.

The Colorado Plateau is one of the most beautiful provinces on our planet. It's an arid province distinguished by deep canyons, distant horizons, and by human reckoning, an air of beauty and mystery that men will fight to preserve. This landscape is carved by rivers and streams that define the Colorado River watershed. The Colorado Plateau has elements of high desert, piñon and juniper woodland, and ponderosa pine forest. It is home to many animal species, including the mountain lion, bighorn sheep, deer, black bear, coyote, and human. Scientists suggest that the first humans entered this province during the late Pleistocene epoch, when much of our planet was encased in glaciers and sea level was more than four hundred feet lower than it is today.

Indigenous peoples continue to inhabit the Colorado Plateau. Their cultures are held in place with great reverence for Mother Earth, and their lifestyles are based on reciprocity with the flow of Nature. Hopi and Navajo are among the peoples who live throughout this landscape. While their languages and lifeways are dissimilar, they share a profound understanding of the spirit of place.

Vernon Masayesva is a member of the Hopi tribe. He is an educator and has served as chairman of the Hopi Tribal Council.

VERNON MASAYESVA: "I think we have to begin the education process, beginning with the kindergarten students, teaching them how important water is. Because in the Hopi way I was taught, Massau [a primary spirit being for the Hopi people] had only three things, he told us. He had a gourd of water, an ear of corn, and a planting stick. He said, 'This is all I have. And my life revolves around these three things. And that if you want to stay here with me, you have to do the same.' That is what we were taught. The corn represents us. People. Our soul. The gourd of water is our connection to the Creator. It is given when you do the right thing. It is a blessing. And the planting stick is a tool. It is technology. So the basic idea is that we have to use technology to keep our environment healthy, if it is sick, to cure it. We have to use technology to keep ourselves healthy, then keep our connections to the Creator strong. Not to sever it. If we don't do this, the technology will go on its own. And it will replace God. And that means we are getting ready for the next world. It means that there is going to have to be a cleansing.

"In the beginning, we followed the Big Colorado River, and spent hundreds of years traveling up the river until we finally came up to the top. There is a point about three or four miles east of the Big Colorado, on the banks of the Little Colorado. A very sacred site we call Sipapuni, which is our emergence. It is our umbilical cord that connects us to our motherland. They [the ancestors] discovered that a person was already living there, because they found foot tracks. So they spent probably many years looking for this person, until they finally found a man working his cornfield. They approached the person and had a dialogue with him. You know like, 'Who are you?'

"'I am Massau.'

"'Is this your land?'

"'No, it is not my land. But I take care of it.'

"Then the question: 'Can we stay here with you?'

"And Massau said, 'That is not up to me. That is up to you people.' And he told them to look around. 'What do you see? You don't see rivers, lakes. It is barren land. So it is a hard place to settle, and to build a permanent civilization. It is poor, and yet it is rich. So if you decide to stay, that would be your decision.'

"So they finally agreed that they would stay.

"So Massau says, 'Then you have to help me steward this land.' And they agreed to a covenant. So we decided that we would live with Massau, help steward the land, live according to his law.

"Massau said, 'You have to fulfill your destiny. And if you live according to the laws that I have given you, you will be blessed. You will live a long time.'

"The Hopis were allowed to settle permanently. They were then told to migrate in all directions, and not to come back to the same place where they met Massau until the wise ones said, 'Now is the time.' And the reason for it was to establish communities all over the Southwest. This was done in expectation of more people to come. So in anticipation of this group of people, Hopis were told to set up villages, which then becomes our history book. We will leave writings on the walls. We will learn from those writings, which clan was there, which direction they were moving.

"Now, if you fly over the Hopi land, you will see the western boundary. It is a snake. It is a river. It is called Colorado River. Then towards the south, another river. That is the Little Colorado River. And then it ends up on a mountain range. Chusca Mountains, we call it now. Then a river snakes north [Chinle Wash]. And then it reaches another river, the San Juan. Then the San Juan joins the Big Colorado River. Now within this area, Hopis call it 'the plaza,' the heart-center of the world, literally. Because Hopis were told this is where the last stage of the civilization will be played out. And that is why to Hopis, this region is very important."

Annie Kahn is a respected member of the Navajo tribal community. She lives near the Lukachukai Mountains east of Canyon de Chelly.

ANNIE KAHN: "Since I'm a Navajo, I know the land very well. And I feel very, very good on the land. I always look forward to get up in the morning so I can see the mountains and the valley. And that is an immediate blessing when I wake up. This is not true if you live in the cities. They are just like canyons. But you are not allowed to see real mountains. You are not allowed to walk on the Earth. There is cement everywhere. You don't live very long that way. You get sick. And that is not real living.

"Before the real sheep come, we had what we called mountain sheep. Mountain goats. These animals were very wild. We know they are good. We know they are delicious. We know that they go with the wind. We know that they walk high mountains. We know that they are very spiritual. They leap high, and with grace. And so before the coming of Spaniards, we huddled together as a tribe and we prayed for the sheep to come. Of course in our mind, we see the mountain sheep. We call it 'rock sheep.' We want to pray to a kind of sacred sheepherder. And this sheepherder that we are speaking of is the one looks after the mountain sheep and mountain goats. So in our minds, we pray to that particular sheepherder. And we say, 'Share your meat with us. We would like to have some in our own backyard so that we can care for them and in return they will feed us. This caring that you do for your mountain animals, we like that idea. Can you share with us?'

"And when we did this in our prayers, we had a spiritual vision that it would come. The new people will come. And they will bring their sheep with them. And so we prayed. And when they came, they brought their guns. Of course we weren't praying for the guns. We weren't looking for chaos. We were looking for sheep to come. But when they came, it belonged to these people. We know that that is ours. We went out there, negotiated with them. Somehow they were very careless. And some of these animals escaped, or they got left behind. So we caught them and cared for them. And we raised them. That is how the second domestic animals come to join us."

Shonto Begay is an internationally recognized Navajo artist and poet who has lived outside his culture, but has returned to his homeland. Shonto grew up near Black Mesa which is regarded by Navajos as the body of the Female Mountain.

SHONTO BEGAY: "My grandfather always said, 'You are but a small part of the puzzle in this huge mystery. You are no greater than the clouds. No greater than the little ant crawling here. No less than either one. Everything is balance. Everything is the way it should be. And to disturb one, to remove one sends ripples out, both in the physical and the spiritual. And it comes back to you in some form.' It is a very powerful vision I grew up with daily.

"My whole world was my horizon. Nothing else existed beyond that. My world is what nurtured me. It is what gave me strength in life. And my whole prayer echoed from one valley to the other and back again. And up into the sun. This was a fantastic place. And I knew every arroyo in the valley, almost every ghost it holds. And the Mother was always there. My real Mother. The Earth Mother was always trod upon very lightly. And everything we do, every teaching that we are given, every story, every song, everything we do had to do with that. About treading lightly. So every place you'd go, you don't go too much in such-and-such direction. Or certain place. And of course we move with the season. That also added a great deal of mysticism, I guess, is what it is. Because I didn't see it, when I went to sheep camp in the summertime.

"So in my view, in the summertime, when I went into the valley, the cornfield, I used to think, if [it were] winter right now it [would] snow. So the Earth itself created great mystery. It was not the skyscraper or a superhighway to really slash my world, or divide my world. Bisected. There was no coal mine. There was no traffic. There was really no supermarket anywhere near that skewed my vision. My world was just a little tiny place with horned toad, coyotes. Occasional dust devils. This is what I was a part of. What I am a part of. And now I am taught to be a part of. And taught to respect. Taught to live with. The wind here in Kayenta is scouring. Very abrasive. Very hot. Sometimes I hear people cursing it and yelling and screaming. I, on occasion, catch myself starting to say things like that. But I know it is all part of this great puzzle, and it is good. Because I lived in the city for a number of years, and experiencing traffic, experiencing smog, experiencing all that negative of the city. I realized, 'Hey, with all the wind, with all the heat and the dryness, with all the harshness, there is a great deal of beauty, and a great deal of holiness here.' It will always be here. I am glad to be back here. After living in the city for a long time."

Herman Atine is a Navajo man who has successfully attended the University of Northern Arizona, but whose true calling is to become a *hataalí*, or Navajo chanter, to help his people maintain harmony and balance within the flow of Nature.

HERMAN ATINE: "Everything here between the earth, the sun, the moon is all related. It is all related to ceremonies, or it is all in the creation stories. Before humans, before we were made, there were only deities, spirits that were in this here world. They are part of being healthy. For us they are part of Nature that we have to use, to get knowledge to take care of ourselves, our family, our relatives, and maybe for our society. It is all part of it. The sun, the earth, the moon, and everything. In our culture we have the benefit of having it in our creation stories. And we can relate back to it to help us be better people, to help us acquire the knowledge to function and have respect for ourselves and everything else.

"After my family, I have just become more of a spiritual person. I have more knowledge, and the spiritual knowledge that I gain makes me feel very happy, and makes me feel good, and makes me be aware of more of Nature. The air, the mountains, the waters, the plants. This is their prayer. This is their song. And for me to have something from Nature—that is very powerful to me, that is the state of mind for me to learn to be a chanter."

Roberta Blackgoat was a highly venerated traditional Navajo woman who lived her entire life on Big Mountain. In the 1970s and '80s, this was the area where 10,000 Navajos faced relocation from their traditional homelands because of interference by political figures within the state and federal governments whose economic concerns continue to subsume their interest in the indigenous members of their constituencies. Ms. Blackgoat was in the vanguard of Navajos who grimly resisted relocation. Remember that Navajo was her primary language, and that she rarely spoke in English.

ROBERTA BLACKGOAT: "The big sacred spot is right here. Where are they going to make a sand painting if they wanted to have prayers, and where are they going to put the Indian baskets? This is the main spot right here. We can't take these baskets or medicines on either side of this sacred mountain. This is a special spot on this Big Mountain and Navajo Mountain or other sacred mountains, they sent words or news or something like that to these sacred mountains. Whatever is happening out here on these sacred mountains, there is a medicine man that uses prayers. And then the winds send the message to these four main sacred mountains. This is how we always say we hate to have these mountains to be destroyed. Because it talks like us in their way. Just like the trees when the wind, the breezes, and you could hear the sounds of it. And even the grasses or whatever the herbs are, they are talking to each other by whispering, or they might be praying. Or they might be singing. That is the song that we hear. If they are destroyed we can't use any medicine out of there. We use medicine and foods. These plants are with us, with some of our medicine and some of our food. And if illness comes around to a person, then we use some strong herbs for it. And they are growing around among us. And here a lot of things have been planned on this area like the mine, or uranium, or oil, or whatever comes up. And they are going to start destroying our medicines. This is the main point that we can't give up. As long as I am here, I am not going to give up. According to our old ancestors, they said, 'Don't ever give up!' There is something going to happen. It is going to happen. It is going to be ruined some day. Either you are going to be shot or whatever, something is going to happen. You are going to be destroyed first, and then they are going to destroy the land."

SHONTO BEGAY: "When we say prayers, we send it off to the mountains' four directions. And we do have Sacred Mountain, within which we call the Holy Land: Dinetah. It is magic because prayers, chants, observing certain ways of life, of living with the earth are observed. Corn grows out of the earth. Food grows out of the earth. People go back to earth. Everything is a cycle. Everything is a circle. Just like the season is a cycle. The year is a cycle. The earth is a cycle. The sun travels in a cycle. Everything is a cycle. So we view things in a cycle. Things happen and happen again. And there is a great cycle that happens that we are a part of. And to destroy something without thinking, plowing a huge piece of land . . . you have this great disturbance. But they [everything in the landscape] are just being taken over. It is amazing.

"When I drive down to Phoenix, every time I go down there, all this tract housing, the condos are just spreading way up in the desert. Where is the water coming from? Probably from Black Mesa. Las Vegas of course. We are just growing as a species. We have become so hungry for our own need, our own conveniences, at the price of compromising other species and the earth itself. Our whole philosophy is that of being a steward of the earth, being just a part of everything. Never taking more than you need. Replacing. Giving to the earth. Offering to the earth. Do your earth ceremony. Not only on Earth Day, but every day. Because it is very, very important. And we live with this every day. Realizing this every day.

"A lot of people believe that we as native people hold the monopoly, I guess, on this environmental thing. Which sort of became almost a fad. I think it is at the core of every culture that I know of. Unfortunately some has been covered up by greed. By money. By other things. It has been covered up by wars. Conflicts. By geopolitical events that are happening. So I think if peace finds its way back, harmony finds its way back, and people decide to live in peace again, everything else will follow. The earth, of course, has to be in there. Making peace. Making peace with the earth. Making peace with the self. That is how we view it."

ANNIE KAHN: "The canyons are a place of refuge, a place where we can go to merge with the wall. In the wall we know that in a sacred manner it opens and it closes. So having that mentality in time of crisis, we wanted to go to the canyon. And to die there that is fine. If there is anything that might happen to us, it was OK to be closer to the canyon than to be caught in the desert. Desert is sort of considered naked. No footholds. But in the canyons there are footholds. And there is a place where the holy ones beckon to come. It seems like in our spiritual destiny is to go to merge with the canyon and the mountain. It is a place the eagles build their nest. It is a place where the eagles raise their sons and daughters. And it is a place of safety. It is dangerous. If these babies fall they may not make it. But the eagles always look for quality of flight and readiness for the time to mature to spread your wings. So it was sheer cliff, but it was all right to jump off, exercise your wings. That was the highest American Indian goal to have thought those thoughts and let it germinate in your brain cells. And let it give birth to your whole body that having that belief and be able to go to the mountains. And be able to endure and fast. No eating. And be able to feel your soul. And that in place of pain you have joy. You are impervious to pain. That is in essence real life."

My friend Roy Kady is a Navajo weaver who has spent his life in the area around Teec Nos Pas in the northeastern corner of the Navajo Nation. He once took me to the *hooghan* where he grew up a mile or so south of the San Juan River. It was here that Roy herded sheep and learned his Navajo lifeway from his grandfather.

ROY KADY: "In a lot of the stories that my grandfather used to tell us in this hooghan that we're sitting in, he said, 'You were given this beautiful language, the beautiful language that you were given when you were born from the east, which is a purity, peace. And then as you grow, the beautiful language that is given to you from the south, the Turquoise language, which is at the age where you're learning a lot of new words and a lot of good words. You're given this beautiful language to talk to people, to be kind in your words, in the way you sound your words, because this is a beautiful language that is given to all of us and that we should never talk harshly among each other, just with everything, with our livestocks and whatever work we do, the people that we meet. Because this language is so powerful in that way that it's also a healing language. It is a gift that is just given to you and can be taken from you if you don't use it the way you're supposed to.'

"That's the language that he talked about, which I totally understand. And there's some people, when they do interviews with me, they would always say, 'That's how your words are. You're calm and your words are very peaceful.' But that's how my grandfather and his teachings were, and that's just the way my mother is also, with whoever she meets. She has very kind words, and those were the only words that were given to us. There were no other words of harshness. So that's the language that was given to us. It's just really sad to see that a lot of the youth, it's not important to them. They don't see the importance of this beautiful language that is given to us. I've heard them say, 'I don't want to talk Navajo.' To me it's very beautiful to know your language because you have that powerful tongue that you can talk and cure people with. It's a healing word and it's really holistic, and everything about our language is very beautiful.

"So in our offerings, in our prayer, we always start with the beautiful language. From here on, may it always be beautiful. And that's why you name the four mountains, the four directional mountains, because that's where we acquired the language. And they're placed in the mountains. That's why we go to these mountains and we make offerings to them on a yearly basis, to continue that.

"To the east we have Tsisnaasjini', which is Blanca Peak and in your early morning offerings, when you say Tsisnaasjini' you're saying, 'In beauty may you surround me with a protection of a rainbow belt to protect me on my track, my daily track or in life.' When you say Tsoodzil, which is the south mountain, Mount Taylor, you're saying, 'Also give me the beautiful language of Turquoise to give me the ability to communicate what I have to communicate today. May my words be all beautiful.' And then our west mountain is Dook'o'oosliid, and when you say Dook'o'oosliid you say, 'From the tip of the peak of San Francisco, may you always have this beam of light to light where I'm going, whether it be day or night. May that beam always be bright for me so that I know my path, where I'm headed.' And then when you say Dibe' Nitsaa, which is the northern mountain, Mount

Hesperus, you're talking about the sacred sheep that we all know is the backbone of the Navajo society. That is a very sacred animal and that's why our fourth sacred mountain is named Dibe' Nitsaa. With that we're strong. The reason why sheep is so important—in a lot of our traditional stories that are told about all the monsters, it was the sheep, the bighorn sheep, that was the sole survivor of all poverty. Everything that has to do with poverty, the bighorn sheep withstood every test, even with the lightning gods. They've tried to strike him down, to cease him. But the bighorn sheep always survived and was the only animal to do that. And that's why the northern mountain stands for that mountain. It's the mountain that gives us strength. It's the mountain that is our protecting mountain. It has a lot of strength, and then that's why it's called Bighorn Sheep Mountain."

Thus, the four sacred mountains spoken of by Roy Kady mark the geomythic parameters of Dinetah, the Navajo homeland. There are other sacred mountains whereon mythic history was enacted. There was the birthplace of Nayanezhghani and Todo Dischinii, the twin heroes of the Navajos who slew many of the monsters. To this day you can see the twins standing guard as geophysical entities throughout Dinetah. Just as the landforms are sacred, so are the plants and animals, and each has an associated story or song. By knowing the stories and songs, and praying in the language of the Diné, the Navajo people remain spiritually affiliated with the biotic community of their homeland.

The Central Arizona Project is one of the most massive public works projects ever undertaken. Its stated purpose is to deliver water to the central valleys of Arizona for agriculture. But in reality, the water is provided to urban centers, including Phoenix and Tucson, so that human communities may grow and flourish in the fragile Sonoran Desert. In order to make the Central Arizona Project function, great concrete canals have been constructed to provide waterways from the banks of the Colorado River to Phoenix and Tucson. This water is moved from the river into canals by great pumps, which are powered by electricity generated many miles to the north by the Navajo Generating Station located on the shores of Lake Powell. This enormous coal-fired power plant is fueled by coal strip-mined from the heart of Black Mesa, the Female Mountain sacred to both Hopi and Navajo peoples. The Central Arizona Project has resulted in massive destruction to landscape, befouling the once crystalline air with exhaust emissions from the power plant, polluting and diminishing the Black Mesa Aquifer upon which both Hopis and Navajos rely for water, disrupting Hopi and Navajo traditional cultures, and greatly impacting the once mighty Colorado River, which is now over-allocated and releases but a few drops of water into the Sea of Cortés. The Black Mesa strip-mining operation, conducted by the Peabody Coal Company of East St. Louis, has long caught the attention of Shonto Begay, Navajo artist and poet.

SHONTO BEGAY: "I did this little painting of the people at the coal mine itself, of Mother Earth compromised, giving away this huge beautiful holy piece of land for the sake of having someone live and breathe in a more convenient space somewhere else over the horizon. One of the pieces I have is this painting here of a young man looking up uttering a prayer, with a corn-pollen bag in one hand, sprinkling corn pollen in the other. The contour overhead is reflected from the water he is standing in. All set over here with an eagle flying. It is just my vision of the time we are in. Living in the later part of the twentieth century, trying to stay connected to the past, to the culture, to the ceremonies, and remain true to the Earth at the same time. And the title of this is 'Into the New World':

> My grandfather's prayers are disturbed.
> In the morning he will walk slowly out the door.
> Sadness upon his once strong face.
> With a slow gait he walks toward the east.
> The blazing sun rises behind the coal mine upon the mesa.
> The air smells of smoke. And that is from cook fires.
> The trampled ground littered with bottles and papers.
> Souvenirs of ceremonies two nights before.
>
> My grandfather's prayer is disturbed.
> The wind that carries his pollen lightly hangs heavy.
> Trucks on the distant highway, blare their impatience.
> Boughs on piñons and junipers are parched brown.
> The rain clouds have abandoned us this summer.
> The watering holes have dried up.
> Up on the mesa machines big as buildings,
> Machines that he has never seen continue to rip into the earth.
> My grandfather's prayer is disturbed.
> The early sky already slashed with jet streams.
> Threads of white, from which no water falls.

Lightning flash of light from jet far above mocks the thirsty earth.
The roar follows far behind.
Laws of nature distorted.

My grandfather's prayer is disturbed.
The ground rumbles slightly as a coal train takes another load away.
Explosives shake the mesa as new veins are opened.
The mesa will be smaller this evening.

My prayers are disturbed.
Still with sprinkled pollen for another day.
Still we have faith.

VERNON MASAYESVA: "I go to these meetings when they talk about the Colorado River. And they talk about the Law of the River and how all these people have an economic interest in it. They have a vested interest. They all look at the river as theirs. It is my river. That is the mentality. That is the mind-set. It is there for me to use. To exploit. To make more money. And I don't want you taking it away from me. So they fight to keep it. It is their water. They forget that the river does not belong to us. That we belong to it. We don't control the river. We think we do. We write laws about it. And it gives us a sense of ownership and control. It controls us. The river controls us. But we don't look at it like that. My hope is that we would change that some way. And I think there is a way to still benefit from the river, to bring the health back to the river. We have taken so much of it, we have got to give something back. That is the Hopi way. Whatever you take, you always give back. You never just take, take, take. You don't say, 'I am separate from the plant or the animal or the stars.' That is why in many of our kachina dances, when we participate with our 'friends' as we call them, we become those things. We have no problem with it. One day I am the moon. The next day I am the badger. I would transform into those things. And it just reinforces the feeling that we are this interconnection here. We are not separate from Nature, but we are all an integral part of it."

iv.

The Sonoran Desert is the most southerly bioregion of the Colorado River watershed. It is one of four deserts contained within the Basin and Range Province, which encompasses much of the intermountain west. The Sonoran is a young desert, barely 10,000 years old. Yet it is the most complex desert ecosystem on the North American continent. It is noted for its lush vegetation, including great columnar cacti, such as the saguaro, which may attain a height of fifty feet, and live for well over a hundred years. The Sonoran Desert is also noted for its abundance of wildlife. Many plant and animal species exist codependently between the peaks of myriad mountain ranges that ripple throughout the province. Humans whose cultures have evolved and existed here throughout the millennia understand that reflecting on this intricate web of life nurtures the spirit of place.

Thousands of years ago, big-game hunters of the Clovis tradition killed mega-fauna for food while this area was yet grassland. Nearly 11,000 years ago, a woodworking culture lived near springs and sometimes slept within rings of stone. It is thought by some that during the Archaic period, about 9,000 years ago, the Sonoran Desert gradually assumed its current form. People hunted small game and gathered wild plants for food. More than 1,500 years ago, the Hohokam people followed trails to the Sea of Cortés where they gathered salt and seashells. They made pottery, lived in villages, and built reservoirs and canals. The Tohono O'odham, or Desert Papago, continue to live here in small communities. They traditionally gathered fruits from the saguaros, and grew beans and melons.

Rosilde Manuel was a highly venerated Tohono O'odham woman who spent her entire life in the Sonoran Desert. For many years, she was the librarian at the Tohono O'odham tribal library in Sells, Arizona.

ROSILDE MANUEL: "My people know this desert as a sacred place filled with life. It is here we learn to love the land. It is said that a long time ago, a mother neglected her baby, in favor of playing a game. The child was taken into the earth, and grew back as a giant saguaro. That is why in our language, a word for saguaro and a word for people is the same."

As mentioned earlier, basket weaving is common to people of many indigenous cultures. Among the desert Indians, baskets are used for gathering, carrying, and storing foodstuffs, including cactus fruits. They are also used ceremonially, and their designs may depict fellow creatures, or even abstract concepts, such as the well-known "man in the maze" motif found on many O'odham baskets. Fillman Bell was born into the Hia-ched O'odham, or Sand Papago, culture. She places great value on the art of basket weaving, and associates this with maintaining the traditions of her people. She recalls much of the basket lore of the desert Indians.

FILLMAN BELL: "This Pima Indian girl told me years ago that her grandmother told her that they used to have to make baskets as tall as people to put in wheat, and corn, and things like that. She said that in order to make one of those baskets like that, one has to stand inside while the other one is [working] on the outside. In one of these sessions she said they felt an earthquake, and the basket fell over, and the woman inside rolled with the basket. I don't know how many years ago that is."

My friend Camillus Lopez is a Tohono O'odham lore master and aural historian who understands the profound importance of mythic motifs that have spiritually sustained his culture even to the present day. It is through the mythic process that metaphor provides intuitive understanding of the relationship of humanity and fellow species to homeland, and casts light on the evolution of consciousness. An exquisitely beautiful symbol associated with O'odham culture is "the man in the maze."

CAMILLUS LOPEZ: "If you look at it real close, the man in the maze, you look at it the way it is now with the opening on top. You would have to go all the way around, and then come into the life. Whereas the other way, where it is the right way, with the opening from the bottom, it is your life. You are going into it. Now that first journey is a straight journey from the hole to the middle part. And the middle part is the death spot. The place where death is. But in O'odham when you say *mu*, that means death, but that doesn't mean the end. It doesn't mean you stop. It only means that something else is coming after that. You follow that entrance into the first part. That is where you are living in your mother's womb until you hit that black spot. Now that black spot has always fascinated me because long, long before, I had asked one of my grandfathers what death looked like. And what my grandfather was saying is that death is an exact replica of who you are, to look at death is to look at yourself, just like your shadow. Your shadow does what you do. You can't lose it. And then when you die, you lay down and there is no more shadow."

Danny Ortiz is a Tohono O'odham elder. One morning shortly after sunrise, he and I sat in the desert sand west of a palo verde tree. Danny had sung a song celebrating the sacred quality of life in his homeland. He then told me something of the traditional ways of his people.

DANNY ORTIZ: "My elderly mother used to tell us we have to be industrious because to be a good worker was something valuable in the old culture. Nobody likes a lazy person. To be a worker, you're useful to your community, to your family, and to yourself. To be an early riser has a very important value, to get things done and to not sleep late. In the summertime out here in the desert, you got up early and do many of your chores before it got too hot, and then you could rest later on. And you ask for good health, because long ago people lived a healthy life. Their diet was healthy eating off the land. The animals we hunted—the rabbit, the pack rat, the mule deer, the javelina, the other animals that helped us survive—we didn't simply kill an animal. We killed for our survival. Some people used to say that when you killed the deer, you spoke to the deer spirit to tell why you make the kill so we as people can survive.

"One of the things we never bother is the owl. We have a lot of respect for the owl. People used to say in the old culture that when we die our spirit will come back in the form of the owl. Everybody respects the eagle. We too have that respect for the eagle. We say that it is the most powerful of all the bird people. The feathers are used for different things. A medicine man will keep a deer's tail for a curing ceremony. If we do something wrong to certain animals, we might get sick later on and would have to have a curing ceremony. The medicine man would use a deer tail, the owl feather, or even little carved figures to imitate the horny toad or other figures.

"As children we were told to leave certain things alone like the horny toad. We always had respect for the horny toad. We never picked it up. We just left it alone. Even like the woodpecker. We never bothered the woodpecker. They would scold us as children if we threw rocks at the saguaro like little kids do. They would say, 'Leave the person alone. You're hurting the person.' I didn't understand. I didn't know as a little kid, but now I know why they said that. Because there is a story about how the first saguaro came to be, came from a person.

"Even the rabbit—after we cook it and eat it, we're told to wash our hands for a certain reason. Things like that we have respect for. The things that we planted, we had to pray, we had to sing, we had to dance and do a ceremony to bring the rains. And that's why the saguaro fruit is very important because from the fruit we make the syrup. Each family donates some of the syrup to the ceremony house where this brew is made. I don't compare it to beer, it's not that potent. After it ferments and sits in the roundhouse for two days and two nights, we drink it. It's a ceremony we go through. Again, it's all the call for rain because the Earth needs the rain. The plants need the rain, the desert animals need the rain. And of course, we as people need the rain. When the rains came, the monsoons, that's when we planted. We got our water from the rains. We grew our squash, our beans, our corn. You see, all those things we ate back then, we were eating healthy and we were active people. Before the coming of the horse, we walked, we ran across the desert and we kept ourselves healthy that way by being very active and eating healthy. But through time that has changed."

CAMILLUS LOPEZ: "There are the medicine people that we call, in the birds and the snakes and everything. There are certain ones that bring certain powers, and some of them are the frogs. The frogs bring rain. They are called after the rain people. When there is a rain, and you sit outside, and there is no music, and the lights are all off, and the sun has gone down, and there is just that crimson, you listen to the frogs at the pond. They are talking to each other. They are talking this frog talk, and it is beautiful to our people, because it brought rain. Long before we had faucets and water tanks, this was the most beautiful sound that people looked forward to hearing. So there is a song about the babies, the frog babies. New life. New songs. So it is asking the children of the frogs, they are saying that maybe you might know a song to teach us. So they are not just singing their beautiful music. They are asking.

"When the first flood came and destroyed the people, I'itoi [an O'odham deity] had created the flood, so he put himself in it. And Coyote, he knew he was going to die too. So he made a raft with reeds tied together, and he was going to sit on that. And the turkey buzzard flew up to the top of the sky and grabbed up onto the top with all the other birds. They grabbed onto the sky and they hung up there. So when the big rain came it flooded the whole place. And they [I'itoi and Coyote] were floating there for many days. And they had made a pact that whoever came out first would be called the Elder Brother. So they floated for many days. After the water had subsided, the waves weren't moving anymore. Wherever they slept wasn't moving anymore. That woke them up. And the Coyote came up first. And I'itoi came up at the Baboquivari Peak. I'itoi made a home there at Baboquivari in that place where he had landed. And that's how his house was then. So then after, he decided to look for Coyote.

"Coyote had been looking for him for a while. And he was yelling out, calling out to see if I'itoi was still alive. And then way over there I'itoi heard it and then he called back. And then they kept calling back and forth. And then they met someplace. And when they had met at that place, I'itoi had pronounced himself to be the Elder Brother, even though Coyote had made it first. But I'itoi doesn't talk like us. He talks backwards.

"If you would boil everything down, you are only earth, fire, water, and air. So everything is connected to everything else. There is Baboquivari. That is where I'itoi lived. That is what is sacred about it. But in O'odham culture, every mountain is sacred. Every mountain has its story. When you share a song about that mountain, you don't say it is any better than any other mountains. There are no levels, no degrees to more sacred or less sacred. It's that every mountain, every little sand, every wash is sacred. It has a story behind it. That is why it was made. If there was no reason for it to be, then it wouldn't have been made. So every mountain has sacredness, its reason for being.

"The great thing about him [I'itoi] was he was one of the creators. He was the one that created O'odham-Hohokam, the ones that were here before. And he is the one who was the greatest medicine man of all. He had the greatest power. But he is not treated apart from O'odham. Just like in other cultures they have their gods. In O'odham, I'itoi lives among us. He is one of us. And he is still here—little stories are told about him doing stuff even today. There is a lady I met, just recently, that said that I'itoi came and tickled her heel. And so she turned around to kick what she thought it was, and here was I'itoi. So she chased him out to catch him. And he took off, and she couldn't catch him. Little green man. But he is one of us. He is not removed from us. He makes mistakes like we do. He has human emotion, everything. And the way that it is described, he is a little man, greenish in color. And he has long hair. The reason he is green, the way it was described to me by my grandfather, was that when kids play in the grass, they will get up and their trousers will be green where they were playing in the grass. And I'itoi, when he did stuff, people would chase him down. And he is a little guy. So he ran through these bushes really fast. And they [the bushes] would slap him. And as he is running really fast, it started turning his skin into a greenish color because that is how he travels is he runs fast through the bush. So running through the bush turned him to green. So that is why he is green."

The people of different cultures who live out their lives in the Sonoran Desert share a community of practice based on their love of the land. The land is seen to be sacred. It is a fragile and arid landscape, and harbors a complex and distinguished biotic community.

Since the early 1990s, the International Sonoran Desert Alliance (ISDA) has been an active grassroots organization working throughout the region to forestall degradation of this fragile habitat due to extractors, developers, and others who are intent on turning habitat into money. ISDA is a coalition of indigenous Native Americans, Mexicans, Anglos, and others who are dedicated to preserving the fragile Sonoran Desert.

Ethnobotanist and author Gary Paul Nabhan is a scientist who has the ability to see a biogeographic region as a complete system. He is also deeply motivated to protect and preserve habitat. Here he addresses the presence of the ISDA.

GARY PAUL NABHAN: "You have a nonprofit organization that is incorporated on both sides of the border planning the destiny of their region that won't make much room for carpetbaggers. We are pinning the landscape down. We are telling the mining companies, 'No, you can't do that. That is a sacred ceremonial ground of the O'odham people. And all of the other cultures here are in solidarity with them. We don't want the impact on the aquifer that we share with those people. And we don't want the impact on that indigenous culture that may not be numerically abundant, but nevertheless is precious to the rest of us.'

"And so you have very odd coalitions happening between city planners, wildlife biologists, human rights activists, green economists, and ecotourism promoters who want to see the integrity of the region intact. It is more valuable intact than it is strip-mined or depleted of its Pleistocene groundwater, or depleted of its vegetation cover. And this coalition has been working. It is functioning in terms of the cross-cultural communication. But it has also repelled a number of threats already. I think the key thing here is it is like developing antibodies for resistance against an invasive disease. The antibodies are already in place. These people can't be walked over anymore. What we have to do is develop enough cross-cultural trust where we say that we are willing to put the places of the heart, the places that mean the most to our cultures on the map, and help one another protect them. And if we show that these places are already cared about, we can repel intrusions within the first month of some lamebrain coming up with this scheme that we don't want in this area."

Amen.

v.

The Río Grande is the fifth-longest river on the North American continent. Over the course of nearly 2,000 miles, the Río Grande descends from its headwaters at an elevation of about 12,000 feet above sea level to the Gulf of Mexico. El Río

Grande del Norte is the lifeline of a mosaic of arid habitats, which nonetheless sustain many diverse biotic communities. The human species has been present within the Río Grande watershed for thousands of years. Long before the Europeans first arrived on this lush continent, Puebloan Indians had established communities along the Río Grande and its tributaries. As mentioned earlier, hunter-gatherers are thought to have gradually crossed the Bering landmass during the Pleistocene epoch at a time when sea level was more than 400 feet lower than it is today. These peoples honed habitat-specific hunting-and-gathering skills, which enabled them to survive in an environment bounded by distant horizons. Over time they evolved communities of practice that allowed them to live in permanent pueblos, the Tanoan-speaking peoples to the north, the Keresan-speaking Indians to the south and west. Here, in the Keresan villages of Acoma and Laguna, the residents practice the cultural skills and ceremonies that continue to celebrate their reciprocity with the spirit of place.

Daisy Velasquez grew up in Encinal, located in the northern part of the Laguna Indian Reservation of New Mexico.

Daisy Velasquez: "My aunt had a barn right next to our place. And there was an old stove there. We used to go stealing eggs from a lady. We would say, 'The rest of you watch. See if that old lady is coming.' And the rest of us, three or two of us would go in the chicken house and steal the eggs. And we would all go back to this farm. And we would put sand in a skillet, and put a little water, and bust the eggs in there and stir it up. So we set the table. And we would sit down to eat. But we couldn't eat the eggs with the sand, because we knew that wouldn't taste good. But we would just sit there and eat our tortillas and drink water. And we would just look at the eggs with sand mixed in.

"When we used to live in Laguna, we were mainly from Old Laguna. My dad is from there. And my mother didn't like living in Old Laguna. She wanted to move up to Encinal. There is a church. And we lived right on the west side. And there is a long building there. A house that my grandmother gave to my mother. And we used to live in there. You know, that was our kitchen. We stayed in there all day long. And then my dad built a big house, just one big room, a big house. A little farther away over from the little house. And we kept our beds. That was our bedroom. That was where we lived. But gradually, later years, my dad added two rooms onto that big building. And then after my mom and dad passed away, well, then my other oldest brother added a dining room and our living room. So it is still up there. It looks new now, because my brother put aluminum roofing up there. And it is made out of rocks. Just rocks. And you won't believe that big room. It stays cool in the summer. That is the coolest place. And it was so high where my brother was going to put on the top. He put mud about that thick [holding her hands a few inches apart]. And that is how he really keeps that place cool. And in the winter it is just warm. It is just really nice and warm.

"We went to trash piles with friends. There were maybe about three, four, five girls you know, about ten or eleven years old. What our favorite was mostly was sardine cans and potted-meat cans. And we would tie them together, and we would make a train with it, and pull them along the road. And we would do things like that. And we would go way, way off from the village. And we would pick cedar berries. And we would build a fire. And we would fry those cedar berries. They were good to eat because they were sweet. We didn't have any toys that came from the store. We really enjoyed playing with things like that. Did you ever see those bowls and plates that were carved like flowers and stuff like that? We used to crayon them around the edges, and those were our decorations. We did a lot of things where we didn't have to buy any toys or anything.

"We used to go piñon picking. You know, where there are a lot of piñons. We used to put grub and our bedrolls on top of a burro. And my mom, and my dad, and my sister, we would go. There is a trail up that canyon. We used to go up. And we would stay maybe three or four days. And you hear, oh the birds, so nice in the morning and in the evenings. And my dad used to get up there and make some kind of noise. And it seemed like the birds just answered back. And when my sister and I used to go off to pick piñons, and we heard birds like that, we used to tell each other to say something to the bird. We used to say those things. And there used to be some wolves sometimes making noise. And we used to get scared. We used to run away. But when we go so far, where they used to have some kind of game. It means fox. It is kind of a song. And it is played in a game. And so we used to always say that: 'Fox, come here, come here.' My grandmother used to sing it. A wolf or a fox, whatever it was, would sit there. And there would be six or seven children, or more or less. We would hold each other. And then pretty soon you just start saying things to that wolf or fox, whatever is sitting there. You just start saying things. 'Oh, you are funny-looking. You have long ears. You got a big nose. You got long legs.' And pretty soon it would get mad, and it would just chase us until it catches us. We would all start running away. That was the game. And when it gets mad it will start chasing us.

"Well, they used to have rabbit hunting every summer. The men and the ladies and their children all go rabbit hunting. They all used to go in wagons. And when a person kills a rabbit, they wouldn't let them chase it on horseback. They have to get off the horse and run for it. And whoever gets there first, that person gets the rabbit. And after four days, they cook something, and they go feed the man that they got the rabbit from. As soon as we start off, we can't drink water. They won't let us, until we get to a place where it is time to have lunch. Then they will let you drink water. You have to stay thirsty.

"Well, we had cattle. My dad had them. So that is why he used to butcher, maybe about two or three in the fall, so that will last us all through winter. And my mom, she used to get a couple ladies to jerk them for us. And they would hang and dry them, and put them away. And before springtime, he butchers about two or three again to last us. After you butcher the cow, you at least let them hang for maybe a day. As long as it is a cold room. That time nobody had no refrigerators. And my mom used to hang them over in the other small house. And they kind of cool off. And then they used to jerk. You just cut them in little pieces like that. And then it is easy to jerk it. You just get a knife and just cut it. Not too thin. Because it if it is real thin, they are easy to break. And then the bones, whatever meat is left on there my dad used to chop them up for my mother, and hang them outside on the line. And when they dry, store them away. And then you cook it to make soup. You know dry bones really taste good if you put hominy in there, or beans, or either dry roast corn. If you put it in, it is good. And red chile. And eating this dry meat, when you pound it, it is really good to mix chile stew, or any kind of stew. It really tastes different from this fresh meat that you make stew. Of course it is good. But gosh. This dry meat really tastes good. And you can just eat. And they jerk the deer meat too. A long time ago when the men used to go out hunting, they never used to bring the deer home like they do. They just jerk it right out there. And they bring it all dry already. Our parents wouldn't have to do the jerking.

"That water was coming from the canyon, the top of the mesa. Encinal. That is where we get all our good water from. It is really good. It is really soft water. Even all these people that live around in these other villages, they go up to Encinal, and haul that water from there for their drinking. We use all that for our irrigation. For corn and wheat and other stuff that our parents plant. They use all that for irrigation. We had plenty of water at those years. But now there isn't that much water.

"It was really nice, those days, and even us as children, we used to go out on the hills and chop wood. I know my sister and I, we used to go out and chop wood when my dad wasn't there. We would go out and chop wood. Then we would come home. We would harness the horses, hitch them to the wagon, and go get the wood and bring it home.

"We had an alfalfa patch down in Laguna. And when he was at the ranch he didn't have time to get it, we would hitch up the horses and come down to Laguna, and my dad used to get men to bale them for him. And they put the bales in the wagon for us. We would take it home. Seemed like everybody those years worked in the field and in small gardens, and everything. And when there was no water to irrigate with, we used to haul our water by buckets from a little river. My sister and I used to haul water. And my dad and my mother used to leave a big tub for us under the fence. We would pour that water in there. My mom and my dad used to get the water from the tub, and water the onions or chile or whatever. Carrots, beets, lettuce, cabbage, corn. And onions, watermelon, melon, pumpkins. They used to grow beans. And pick the fresh beans. And when they dried, pick it and shell them. And my dad used to put a lot of wheat. People used to put a lot of wheat. And they would help one another to cut the wheat. And then when we was through cutting the wheat, when the next person is going to start cutting theirs, they all help. They try to all help one another. Because in those years, nobody said, 'Well, I got to be paid. You got to pay me.' No, everybody did things freely for one another. But these days everybody has got to be paid. They want money. It was nice.

"We really enjoyed a lot of things during my years. We used to go on top of the barns, and you know those corn husks that are purple. We used to pick those. When you chew them they are really sweet and juicy. We really made our own candy too. We did that those years. It was good. We used to shell the piñons and mix it with candy that we made."

Dolores Lewis is a potter who lives near the Acoma Pueblo. Her mother was Lucy Lewis, a celebrated potter born in the early years of the twentieth century. Dolores takes much of her inspiration from her home habitat, which she knows intimately.

DOLORES LEWIS: "I say that I have roots at Chaco Canyon and Mesa Verde, because up to this time, we are able to make similar type of pottery that has been made back then. So I believe that my ancestors did come from these two areas. I guess I was meant to be a potter the day when I was born, because my mother has been a potter all her life. And I have been surrounded with potters all these many years.

And it just came natural for me to take up pottery making. And I have been at it all this time. We gather the clay at Acoma. And it is a sacred place. And no one else is allowed to get it except us Acomas. And there is a clay pit there, and there is enough clay to last until the next generation to use. And we have used the same clay that our grandmothers have used long ago. And it is still there. We have to go hike over there in order to get the clay because it is a very difficult place to get it. And it is a family task, where everybody goes and helps to gather the clay. And the clay comes in slabs. And as soon as the clay hits the air, the clay starts coming apart. So we have to put it out in the sun to dry and get it home. Well, when we go out and collect old potsherds, we come across old designs on the potsherds. So we know that they are from the Anasazi [ancestral Puebloan] era. So we get our inspiration from those old potsherds. So we kind of study them, and we try to figure out how this design was on the pot. So we just go from there. And then we put that on our newer Acoma pots.

"When I go back out to the mesa, I feel at ease because it is like a retreat to me when I go back out to the pueblo. Or when I am out in the valley, or up in the mountains, I feel relief from the outside pressure because there is just so much to see out there. The beauty of the earth and your surroundings. And it is just there. And then it has to be up to you if you want to appreciate what is out there. When I put my design on my bowl, it gives me a relaxation and it gives me a good feeling that I am able to do designs on the pottery. And it gives me a good inspiration because all these designs all pertain back to Mother Nature. When you turn your pottery bowl like this, you are able to put water in it. You are able to put your cornmeal in there. You are able to put food in it. You are able to drink from the pottery. It gives me a good feeling when I start putting my design on. I don't usually just play with it. Because this is my lifetime. It is going to take me up until the day that I am ready to leave the earth. And I am going to leave the earth by taking a piece of pottery like my ancestors did long ago. So I will be able to carry my water in my pottery when I go."

Five hundred years ago, when Europeans first trickled into the Western Hemisphere, the human population of our planet was poised at about 500 million souls. At that time, some demographers estimate that about 75 million people lived on the North and South American continents. Today, our species totals some 6.5 billion souls, having more than tripled over the last century. According to the United Nations Population Division, the human population of our planet Earth will level out at just under 10 billion by the year 2050.

There are myriad factors that have contributed to the success of our species, but some may well contribute to our all-too-imminent demise. In part, since the advent of Western civilization, we have idealized our own species. In so doing, we have separated ourselves from Nature, even pursued a sense of mastery of Nature. We have developed technologies that, while miraculous, have frequently been misapplied. With all our intelligence, we fail to successfully extrapolate future probabilities.

There are still those who live in a state of reciprocity with other creatures, and who perform ceremonies and rites in celebration of Nature's cycles. Their intuitions of something immanent have not atrophied. [In his book, *The Pueblo Indians of North America*] anthropologist Edward Dossier, a native of the Tewa Indian pueblo of Santa Clara, wrote,

> Man alone can disrupt universal equilibrium by thought, word, or deed. The consequences of imbalance are illness, disaster, drought. Rites and ceremonies properly performed keep the seasons moving, allow the sun to rise and set properly, bring rain and snow, and ensure a well ordered physical environment and society.

The traditional Tewa-speaking people who inhabit the pueblos along the northern Río Grande are among those who have lived according to their comprehension of the flow of Nature. They uphold traditions as taught by their ancestors whose lineage extends millennia into the past. They understand the undeniable necessity of honoring the spirit of place.

Four Tewa people indigenous to the region of the Río Grande del Norte provide a glimpse into their cultural perspective: Dr. David Warren, José Lucero, Dr. Rina Swentzell, and Toni Singer, who was a young girl at the time of her interview.

DAVID WARREN: "It is very, very important that all of us realize that we are part of the Tewa world in the sense that we are not only ringed by physical mountain ranges, the Pajarito Plateau, and on the other side by the Sangre de Cristos, but that we really believe in something called quality of life. I think it would be well for us to remember whatever was defined by the earliest people here in defining their universe. The area we live in is a little crucible. It is bounded, and it is shaped, and it is defined by the physical mountain ranges. I think it is within that crucible that for 10,000 years, perhaps even longer, people had learned to live on the margin of many, many kinds of limitations. I think it would be well for us to remember in terms of physical archaeological evidence what happens when you overuse or neglect basic limitations in the human and material resources that define a land that has got very little water. And when it gets it, it gets too much. It has to be retained. It has to be used sparingly and so on. All that seems to boil down to what kind of living patterns were established here. And to my knowledge, the earliest inhabitants built in tufa cliffs where nature already created a Natural self-limiting design as to expansion of the numbers of people. It also provided those kinds of natural catches for the water where the natural areas could be watered and developed as agricultural fields and so forth. And around it all, of course, was another kind of subsistence pattern—hunting and gathering."

José Lucero: "As Pueblo people, or agriculturists, we depend upon the water. We depend upon irrigating. This year my corn had a rough start, and almost didn't make it. We did one month of ceremony, and finally the rains came. And as the rains came, my corn grew about a foot a week, it seemed like. Of course along with it were the weeds. So I had a bumper crop of corn, and a bumper crop of weeds this year.

"We were very blessed by the community involvement of the people. You know, the prayers that are sent up. So one of the ways that we have been able to maintain within this world is the ceremonies, the prayers, which are done through dances by the community people members, clans, extended families. We were able to maintain ourselves along this river. And it has worked. A community of men coming together to put their work in cleaning the ditches, or acequias as they are called by the Spanish. We are able to hold on to the water that we need. And we are dependent upon the rainfall, the snowfall, and the recharge areas. Recharge is very slow, with the amount of people that we are currently getting into our areas. So in the future I see a tremendous drawdown, which has happened in the past, and not so long ago.

"We see some of the ruins that were left by our ancestors—Chaco Canyon, Mesa Verde, Canyon de Chelly, and others, because they were dependent upon the surface flow of water. Now it is a little more intense because we are looking at the drawdown of the underground rivers, or aquifers as they are called."

Rina Swentzell: "The old ancestral people moved through this region for thousands of years. And the intimacy that they developed with the land, I think, is what has kept them going for so long in such a place. Even today, I think we have forgotten that what has helped our people survive for so long is that intimacy that we had with the land, with the place, with the rocks, the mountains. Part of that intimacy, of course, especially in this region, is to know where the water areas are. The water is seen as being absolutely important for life. Without it creation doesn't happen. It is the semen of the father that keeps creation going. But the snaking water through this region, the Río Grande, and of course throughout all of Pueblo mythology, the lakes are very important. All water places are extremely important, because without water we don't survive here. And it is so sparse that they have become very special places. They are also those places in which the energy of the world is very strong because they are also openings of places to go to the underworld, other levels of existence that are openings to the underworld. The Río Grande is a place that is also frightening to the Pueblo people. It is frightening because it comes with incredible power. The power. And that is why I think that we talk about the 'water-wind-breath,' because the power of all creation is there. And it can be in the wind, and certainly in the water, and especially in that strong-flowing water that we know. And the word in Tewa for Río Grande is *Osongue*, the large water place."

JOSÉ LUCERO: "So if you go around some of these sites, here in New Mexico, and Pajarito, and La Bajada Hill, you can see some of the old terracing that was done to conserve the water during a drought period. The Pueblo people learned this because they went through the hardships of surviving those drought years, and then utilizing the semiarid seeds through plant breeding and utilization and trading, from some of the people of the south. So these were in place. So that was what they call today a 'no-till' way of planting. And also dry farming."

RINA SWENTZELL: "The spirit moves through the water. An incredible word that we have for the source of life is something we talk about as that *O-po-wa-ha*, the water-wind-breath. It is there in the water and in the wind that we can see the spirit, that we can see life moving. It is there where the life force is visible, as well as in the clouds, of course. We don't take the life force and put it in a superhuman being, as Christians do with God. That already begins to show us the focus on human beings when you put the life force in a superhuman creature. God is superhuman form. But we keep it within the trees, within the water, within the wind, within the clouds. And we are to move through that context of the water

The Spirit of Place

and the wind, and breathe the same breath. We are breathing the same breath that the rocks do. That *the* wind does. That gives you a totally different feeling. This is it. There is no other reality. We don't go to heaven. We don't leave this dirty world to go to a golden clean heaven. We are here. This is it. This is *the* world. It doesn't get any better than this. We can't take care of it if we think that it is a place to be shunned, and that we have better things to look forward to. And we can't walk respectfully where we are at this moment and take care of things, and touch things with honor, and breathe each breath. That is what that water-wind-breath is about. It is: 'My goodness, I can breathe it in and I become a part of this world.' I mean in no uncertain terms I am a part of this world that I live in every second because I breathe it every second."

JOSÉ LUCERO: "You see the pottery that we have here. The pots are adorned by the water serpent, or the Evañu that is the deity of the terrestrial waters. Not only of the Río Grande, but all the other tributaries that feed it. So traditionally, there are the prayers that go into the art itself. The lightning-cloud symbols are the same—prayers for moisture—many times on an individual artist basis, or as a family, and then as a community, these people continue to follow the designs of the old people. Some of the other symbols—Bear always knows where there is water. So these symbols again appear. Or the prayer feathers, the eagle feathers that are presented. Eagle is a bird that flies the highest. So we have those prayers that are going up and asking for a blessing of thanksgiving, a little bit of rain."

RINA SWENTZELL: "Here, especially in the Southwest, you look around you and you see that horizon—a 360-degree horizon around you. And then you see the blue with the clouds going over you. You are the center. At any point that you stand in the Southwest, you are the center, and you are in containment at any point that you stand. And the Pueblo people really picked up on that. They said, 'Oh, we live within the earth bowl. This is where we dwell. Wherever we are, we are at the center.' And that is what we experience every day. And being at the center, seeing that far horizon with the mountains that contain us in this earth bowl and all the symbolic kiva bowls that the Pueblo people make with the mountains along the rim, it is all about that.

"And then the earth is covered with the sky basket. And you are talking about the marriage between earth and sky. That is exactly what they are talking about. The father and the mother. But it was not in terms, so much, as male and female as it was father and mother, which is a very different concept. Male and female then become included within father and mother. And that is a very different meaning than say, the male sky and the female earth, which brings in real explicit kind of sexuality, which the Pueblo people weren't so much interested in, as in the parental nature of mother and father, within which creation happens. Because it is only when the male and female come together as father and mother and children are produced that creation really happens. This is the creation right now because those two have come around us. In that sense then, Pueblo people talk about community as having mothers and fathers and children. The oldest people always talked about this father, and then their mothers in those communities also. I mean, whether they are your mothers or not. Whether they are your fathers. But then everybody else is children. But those people are also children—the flexibility of roles in that way. The notion of having people who are responsible and nurturing and caring about the entire context that one lives in, it is that kind of model. That was taken from the way they saw the cosmos as being structured. That's the way the cosmos are ordered. It is within that context that we live."

DAVID WARREN: "I think that the other part of it is that those early inhabitants were very clear about what they had to do to preserve the shrine systems that were on tops of the mountains and still are there today, and still used. And keep them from being even approached in terms of permanent living systems, dwellings, or inhabited areas. In other words, they left sacred space. But the sacred space was everywhere, from one mountaintop to the other, and everything between. It reminds one, every day, when one looks at what Alfonso Ortiz calls the Tewa World, in both vertical dimensions as well as horizontal planes, it reminds one that you are in a very unique place when you live in this part of the country. It has limitations, and you must care for that environment. If you betray it, it will destroy you."

TONI SINGER: "When I go up the canyon I like to see how the trees blow, and how the leaves fall in the water. It looks neat. And sometimes I play with the leaves in the water. Make pictures. I like nature. There are a lot of things to do. And the best part of it is, I like to see the water flow and how it sounds. It is fun to get out in the wild."

JOSÉ LUCERO: "You can't separate one from the other—the environment, the culture. Many people call it religion. It is a way of life. It is what people do on a day-to-day. It is every day. They have to go hand in hand, working with plants, with the animals. It is within the ceremonial year, that different things take place. Now we are into the winter ceremonies. Giving thanks for the animals. We have done our harvest dances, and thanksgiving of clouds, and others that have brought us this far, so it is a continuous cycle. It is an ongoing cycle. And we are blessed today that we are able to have our community, or our children, or grandchildren and the uncles, and we are just kind of moving up the step. As we get older we say, 'Oh, that is going to take a long time, being a grandfather.' It is a reaffirming that we have just kind of moved up a notch. When we get beyond a hundred, then we are born again. And we start over. And when we leave, I think there is more work."

RINA SWENTZELL: "Elders in those communities played a very important part because they felt themselves to be connected. And I think that if things work in union, if older people don't have a sense of their own meaning and their own sense of place within community, which I think a lot of people have lost within all communities, then other people can't relate to them that way. When any culture can't just honor somebody because they are sixty-eight years old . . . but that that sixty-eight- and that eighty-eight-year-old person has something that flows out of them anyway. And that means that they have had a lifetime in which they have thought about things, and that they have been careful about things. And then they really can be people who can begin to put their arms around other people. And if they don't have that capability within themselves, then we are really all lost. Because we need those older people to be coming around us, and telling us, 'Now stop. Listen. Look around you. You are acting too fast. Is this appropriate for where everybody else is, including where the clouds are? Is this what we should be doing?' I mean, it just seems right for old people to be taking on that role. But what happens to people who don't grow up ever experiencing that for themselves? Then how can they do that for other people? And I think that a real dilemma we have is having generations of people who don't know how to behave like that. And then how can they be older people who other people can respect?"

TONI SINGER:

> My name sits
> on a soft, smooth lake.
> My voice sounds like
> gentle rain
> falling from the sky, hitting me

like hard strong lightning.
When the cold wind comes,
I will flow
from place to place.
My name is soft,
soft like a big flat quilt.

A few winter days pass,
singing birds are looking
for juicy worms,
blooming flowers grow.
Life comes back
back into me.
Flowers grow,
and trees fall on me.

I am *P'oekwín Póví*
I am Lake Flower.
If you look into me
you will see
a beautiful person.
You will see yourself.

RINA SWENTZELL: "The dances that still happen—one of the primary things that is happening is that we are actually communicating with the clouds. It is a way of moving our bodies so that the energy, and its energy communication is what we are going to take from it.

"What I have been thinking a lot about with community is that we have gotten too small a definition of community. I go back to Pueblo thinking because there, community really was not just a human community. It included the place within which we lived, so that the mountains were part of community. The water was part of community. Trees, rocks, plants. You couldn't move through any day in that old world, even when I was growing up, without knowing that you were part of that whole community of trees, rocks, people. Today we just talk about human community, and it gets to be such a small thing within the larger scope of things. We keep making the world smaller and smaller until it is nothing but *us*. It's just human beings. Out of context. Out of our natural context. Out of our cosmological context. We have become so small in our view of the world. Our world is simply us, human beings. That is a crucial thing that we need to get beyond and move back again to seeing ourselves within context."

Interlude

Shifting Coordinates

T HE AMERICAN SOUTHWEST may be perceived as an eco-systemic sphere of reference
filled with myriad landforms, life forms, waterways, and cloud forms that have
helped shape human perspective for thousands of years. This mythic landscape is
tinted with hues that emanate from the living Earth long associated with local
deities who have danced here since time out of mind. Today's economically driven
paradigm of turning habitat into money not only devastates geophysical and at-
mospheric environments, it also results in the "opaque-ing" of the lens of mythic
perspective, thus thwarting our intuitions of an immanence inherent in our
planet.

Cultures indigenous to the American Southwest have evolved in ways com-
mensurate with both physical and spiritual survival in this most arid of North
American habitats. Their partnership with homeland is characterized by recognition of our species as part of, rather than separate from, this landscape we co-
inhabit with our fellow species. Myth and ritual continuously evolve within the
context of homeland.

According to their creation myth, the history of the Hopi people begins in
this world with their emergence from an earlier world through the Sipapuni that
is located near the Little Colorado River upstream from the confluence with the
Colorado River. After wandering through this arid landscape for some time, the
Hopis encountered Massau, a spirit being with whom they formed a sacred
covenant. They promised Massau to live in what is now their homeland as stew-

ards, to annually perform the seasonal cycle of ceremonies, and thus remain in harmony with the spirit of place.

Throughout their mythic history, the Hopi people have complied with the covenant established between their ancestors and Massau. Long ago, they created annual rituals wherein they invoked the deities to bring rain and provide them with the spiritual and physical sustenance to flourish in a harsh environment. Their ancient villages are still situated on three great promontories that extend southwestward from the main body of Black Mesa, a landform sacred both to themselves and to the Navajo people whose nation totally surrounds the Hopi Nation.

Both the Hopi and Navajo peoples have a strong sense of cultural mythic history in the American Southwest. The mythological motifs permeating both Hopi and Navajo cultures were wrought from within a homeland that may indeed be geo-mythically mapped. The landforms and waterways are themselves sites where the local deities continue to interact with their indigenous peoples. For example, the San Francisco peaks are sacred to the Hopis inasmuch as the peaks are home to the *katsinas*, those spiritual beings who appear in ritual dances throughout the annual cycle of ceremonies celebrated in the Hopi villages. By comparison, Mount Ararat, located in what is now Turkey, is a mountain sacred within the Judeo-Christian mythic tradition as the landing site of Noah's ark, the vessel from which all species survived the great Flood, thence repopulated the earth.

Four centuries ago, Spanish colonists penetrated the watershed of the Río Grande del Norte and gradually settled into a state of semi-reciprocity with the Río Grande Puebloans and Comanches. Well over two centuries ago, transplanted Anglo culture was focusing on claiming as much of North America as possible for a new nation wherein "all men are created equal, that they are endowed by their Creator with certain unalienable Rights, that among these are Life, Liberty, and the pursuit of Happiness." These words were penned for America's Declaration of Independence by Thomas Jefferson, himself a slaveholder, who was concurrently sculpting his agrarian vision for American culture. In his *Notes on Virginia*, Jefferson writes:

> Those who labor the earth are the chosen of God, if ever He had a chosen people, whose breasts He has made His peculiar deposit for sub-

stantial and genuine virtue. It is the focus in which He keeps alive that sacred fire, which otherwise might escape from the face of the earth.

Jefferson did not anticipate that his agrarian vision was soon to be supplanted by the Industrial Revolution. Even so, this vision was to become an important factor in the shaping of American land-use policy. In her paper "US Land Use Policy and the Commodification of Arid Land (1862–1920)," economist Lisi Krall points out:

Jefferson helped to put in place the legal basis of land ownership and establish a systematic method of surveying land to augment it. More-over, he worked to displace precapitalist land institutions embodied in the economies and cultures of Native Americans, and he fully supported economic liberalism and its prescripts for trade, specialization, and the rights of individuals to pursue their interests.

Within a century, a one-armed Civil War veteran by the name of John Wesley Powell had run the Colorado River and mapped the arid lands of the West. Powell's thinking reflects residual components of Jefferson's agrarian vision in the following excerpt from his testimony for the House Select Committee on Irrigation, March 15, 1890:

Let the General Government organize the arid region, including all the lands to be irrigated by perennial streams, into irrigation districts by hy-drographic basins. . . . Then let the people of each such irrigation district organize as a body and control the waters on the declared irrigable lands in any manner which they may devise.

Powell had previously passed through Hopi and Navajo country, and had mapped their respective watershed as the Río Colorado Chiquito drainage dis-trict. Much of the intermountain west receives less than ten inches of annual pre-cipitation and is frequently perceived as a wasteland in the eyes of those more accustomed to greener pastures. While it was apparent to Powell that the hun-dredth meridian divided the verdant East from the arid West, a coterie of east-ern land speculators wished it otherwise. Men like William Gilpin—described by Marc Reisner in *Cadillac Desert* as "the prototypical Renaissance man of the American West: soldier, philosopher, orator, lawyer, geographer, author, windbag and booby"—were starstruck by the development potential for turning the West into a haven for humanity, American-style. Just east of the hundredth meridian, Kansas was boasting an annual rainfall of more than forty inches per year—four times greater than many of the desert regions a few hundred miles to the west. Horace Greeley coined his famous piece of advice: "Go West, young man. Go West!"

Hence, the stage was set for the enormous surge of applied techno-fantasy and construction that was to befall the Colorado and other western rivers during the twentieth century that resulted in public works projects conceived by four or five generations of minds honed by the Industrial Revolution. The western land-scape came to be commodified, many of its denizens supplanted, its resources fair game. A new layer came to mantle the watersheds of the American West, its prevailing hue the color of money.

Part II of *Healing the West* focuses on development of the Colorado River, the aquatic lifeline of the American West throughout the twentieth century, and glimpses the evolution of the currently prevailing economic paradigm, a paradigm that is contrary to the traditional indigenous points of view nurtured by a reverence for the flow of Nature.

Moving Waters:
The Colorado
River and the West

ALL ORGANISMS have descended from the same distant ancestral life form. . . . Because of this single ancestry, which arose on Earth over 3.5 billion years ago, all species today share certain fundamental molecular traits. . . . Because all organisms have descended from a common ancestor, it is correct to say that the biosphere as a whole began to think when humanity was born. If the rest of life is the body, we are the mind. Thus, our place in nature, viewed from an ethical perspective, is to think about the creation and to protect the living planet.

—Edward O. Wilson
  The Future of Life

⇒ H IGH AND DRY IN DESERT COUNTRY—to my mind, there's nothing better. For half a century I've been wandering through the intermountain west and deep into Mexico, endlessly intoxicated by the intricate weave of geophysical, biological, and cultural diversity that forms the ever-changing mosaic that overlays this part of the North American continent. In my mind's eye, I can visualize vast spans of arid landscape that lie west of the hundredth meridian, a habitat that is often drier than a dead man's bones.

To this day, I continue to ponder the United States Department of the Interior Geological Survey map prepared by Nevin M. Fenneman in 1964 that is affixed to my bathroom wall, which portrays the geophysical divisions of the contiguous forty-eight states. I'm incessantly drawn to what is defined as the intermontane plateaus division of the continent that separates the Rocky Mountains to the east from the Sierra–Cascade ranges to the west. The intermountain west extends from just south of the Canadian boundary to deep into Mexico, and cradles three distinct geographic provinces.

To the north lies the Columbia Plateau that includes parts of eastern Washington, Oregon, and western Idaho. The landscape here is arid yet falls within the Snake–Columbia watershed that drains enormous quantities of water into the Pacific Ocean. In the middle of the intermountain west is situated the roughly circular Colorado Plateau whose watershed is comprised of the Green, San Juan, Escalante, Colorado, and other rivers whose main stem once emptied into the

Sea of Cortés. Wrapped around the western, southern, and eastern aspects of the Colorado Plateau is the Basin and Range Province, so named because the landscape is characterized by myriad mountain ranges separated by basins. This province is home to the four North American deserts—the Mojave, the Great Basin, the Sonoran, and the Chihuahuan. Watershed-wise, the Great Basin desert of Nevada and western Utah is a closed basin. The Mojave and Sonoran deserts lie within the Colorado River watershed, while the Chihuahuan Desert and the arid plateaus to the north drain into the Río Grande, which traditionally empties into the Gulf of Mexico.

This is the landscape that I love. I've wandered its wildlands for decades, camping in remote canyons or on mesa tops far from fellow humans. I've slept for thousands of nights beneath the open sky, my last waking moments spent staring into the starlit firmament, the wind carrying away my thoughts and contemplations. When I close my eyes, I can picture this enormous landscape that extends hundreds of thousands of square miles. I recall scores of adventures with great friends, many of whom have since passed from this world. My perspective has been shaped and reshaped as I've wandered forth, almost always packing recorder and microphones in my kit, the better to hear voices crying, singing, or laughing in the wilderness, or communities and villages, and even cities from time to time. I have witnessed great change in the multifaceted West since I first entered the Mojave Desert half a century ago.

As the great nineteenth-century philosopher Henry David Thoreau wrote, "The mass of men lead lives of quiet desperation"—this at a time when the human population of our planet was but a sixth of what it is today. Presently there are a lot more men (and women), and we indeed live in desperate times. Our species has exceeded the carrying capacity of our planet to sustain us, at least at the level at which we currently extract. Our numbers will have to decrease either by natural attrition or by virtue of disaster if our biological species and many others are to survive.

I have pondered this alone and have discussed it endlessly with many of my gifted friends, all of us carefully nurturing the last vestiges of our guarded optimism with quiet desperation.

And thus it came to be that in 2001, thanks to my good friend Craig Newbill, director of the New Mexico Humanities Council, and through grants from the National Endowment for the Humanities and the Ford Foundation, I was given the opportunity to produce a six-part radio series entitled *Moving Waters:*

The Colorado River and the West. This project enabled me to reexamine a major watershed with which I was long familiar. I worked in part with Nancy Dallette, who was coordinator of the larger project that involved a traveling exhibition and other components. In the main, I worked alone, attempting to create a model of what Garrett Hardin regarded as "ecolate thinking," extrapolating future possibilities from existing data. I traveled throughout the watershed visiting the headwaters of the Green, Colorado, and San Juan rivers, and the delta at the north end of the Sea of Cortés in northwestern Mexico. I interviewed dozens people whose points of view represent many perspectives—scientists, ranchers, Indians, Mormons, bureaucrats, "water buffaloes," folklorists, farmers, concerned citizens, poets, writers, historians, lawyers, environmentalists, scholars, former secretaries of the interior—each of whom provided me with their thoughts and insights, their collective sense of the watershed, that I might excerpt and weave into an overview the complexity of a watershed that is greatly over-allocated.

In the section that follows, I've included the transcribed narrative from the radio series amended only by my written connecting narrative for purposes of clarity. I've also included narrative and other material that I've written or gathered over the last thirty-eight years that casts light on the Central Arizona Project, which spawned the "greatest water war in American history" and, in my mind, stands as the perfect model of environmental folly and catastrophe.

The Colorado River, the aquatic lifeline of the American West, has suffered a century of techno-fantasy. When producing the radio series, I did my best to be an objective documentarian and hold my biases at bay. However, writing this book requires me to follow my seat-of-the-pants intuition and say it the way I see it. And the way the Hopi Indians saw it as their sacred homeland, Black Mesa, began and continues to be strip-mined for coal to fire the power plant to generate the electricity to pump water out of the Colorado River and into the valleys of central Arizona. Thus we have the perfect model of the American economic paradigm for turning habitat into money, a paradigm that is antithetic to the points of view expressed in the first half of this book.

i.

The Colorado River watershed spans parts of seven western states, including the entirety of Arizona and part of Mexico. Myriad tributaries contribute to the main stem of the Colorado River. The Green River, whose headwaters lie within the southwestern quadrant of Wyoming, empties into the Colorado downstream from Moab, Utah. The Green River is fed by several major tributaries, including the Big Sandy, Little Snake, Yampa, Duchesne, White, Price, and San Rafael rivers. Another major tributary of the Colorado is the San Juan River, whose headwaters lie above Pagosa Springs, Colorado. The Animas River enters the San Juan near Farmington, New Mexico. Other tributaries to the main stem of the Colorado include the Gunnison, Dolores, Dirty Devil, Escalante, Paria, Little Colorado, Virgin, Bill Williams, and Gila rivers.

The greater Colorado River watershed encompasses a drainage area of more than 244,000 square miles, and the main stem of the river is about 1,440 miles long. In the main, this watershed is borne in an arid landscape that nonetheless was homeland to various indigenous peoples for well over ten millennia prior to the coming of Europeans in the sixteenth century. Spanish conquistadores and colonists first entered what is now the American Southwest in the 1500s, mainly following El Camino Real de Tierra Adentro (the Royal Road to the Interior) that closely parallels the Río Grande del Norte, whose watershed lies immediately east of the Colorado River watershed. These watersheds are separated by the Continental Divide, east of which water flows into the Atlantic, and west of which, the Pacific. There are points along the Continental Divide where you may stand with one foot in each watershed. The yield of the Río Grande is about one tenth that of the Colorado River, while the yield of the Colorado is but a modest fraction of that of the Columbia River system, the mightiest river that spews forth west of the Continental Divide in the lower forty-eight states.

The first thorough and systematic exploration of the Colorado River watershed was conducted by John Wesley Powell, the one-armed Civil War veteran who was part adventurer, part scientist, and part bureaucrat. William deBuys, in his excellent book *Seeing Things Whole: The Essential John Wesley Powell*, says:

> Virtually alone among his late nineteenth century contemporaries, [Powell] saw that the character of western lands would shape—and in turn be shaped by—the way in which those lands were settled. He further saw that the result of that interaction would ramify onward for generations and would have profound consequences for the land and for

American society. Powell was America's first great bioregional thinker, and the lessons he taught we are still at pains to learn.

Powell and his men floated through the Grand Canyon in wooden dories to an unknown destiny, a grand adventure that required courage, resolve, and great physical stamina. Powell was followed by an influx of easterners who looked at the arid West and envisioned fortunes to be made if only the landscape could be made verdant. By the beginning of the twentieth century, entrepreneurs were poised to rearrange the American West (while filling their moneybags) at the expense of the natural watershed. One hundred years of Colorado River history reads like a cross between science fiction, the financial pages of the *Los Angeles Times*, a lawyer's dream, and an environmentalist's nightmare from which we are trying to awaken.

One would do well to realize that if one filled a glass of water in Los Angeles or San Diego, or Phoenix, Denver, Provo, or Albuquerque, it is probable that at least part of the water in that glass would come from the Colorado River system. It is a small river, but without it, many of the cities of the West and most of the irrigation districts would never have developed.

The Colorado River provides water for 25 million of us throughout the West. Just think of that! How many of us realize that during the last century, waters from the Colorado River and its tributaries have been dammed and redirected to meet the needs of folks throughout seven western states and northwestern Mexico. By human standards, it has come to be regarded as the aquatic lifeline of the Southwest. However, the Colorado River serves a much larger biological community of species in which the human species is but a single member. We should regard the Colorado River not as a commodity closely associated with money but rather as the lifeblood of the landscape in which it is cradled, through which it has carved the most intricate and spectacular system of canyons in the world, and within which it nourishes an ever-shifting mosaic of countless ecosystems that remained biologically interact over geologic time. For thousands of years, members of our own species interacted harmoniously within the larger biological community. While we can never return to the Edenic milieu of our ancestors, it is imperative that we re-invoke that system of sensibilities and intuitions through which we shall recognize our kinship with every species that has ever lived on our planet, and once again act accordingly.

Hiking the ancient trails of the Colorado Plateau, one can stumble across artifacts created by people from cultures that have long since disappeared. Human beings have inhabited the North American continent for at least twelve millennia. It is interesting that just about every culture or civilization envisions an environment appropriate for its respective creation myth—whether it is the Garden of Eden or the Grand Canyon.

Phillip Tuwaletstiwa is a Hopi Indian who is extremely sophisticated in the ways of modern America. For many years, Phillip was the assistant director of the United States Geographic Survey. As a trained geodesist, he is aware of his precise location wherever he happens to be. However, when it comes to his Hopi homeland, he recognizes the landscape as both a geophysical and geo-mythic environment, perceived within the context of spatial coordinates as well as through the lens of mythic perspective. As a result, he is acutely aware on both intellectual and intuitive levels of the way his people understand their cultural relationship to their homeland.

PHILLIP TUWALETSTIWA: "There are hundreds of shrines all over northern Arizona and southern Utah and southern Colorado that are connected in our minds and our consciousness. And we think of them not in terms of 'it takes so many hours to drive there.' We think of them in terms of 'what do they mean to us as a tribal people.' We know this clan was here, that clan was there. We know that this is the place where you go to get a particular mineral, an herb, a particular plant. We are familiar that something happened there a long time ago that affected us. We worry about these places, that they are not desecrated. They are not hurt. We feel protective of them. I think of Mesa Verde. I think of it as a connection, as an important Hopi place.

"But it is more than being Hopi. I think the nearest analogy that we have now would be the World Trade Center. Because [its destruction] affected all of us. Native Americans. Hispanics. Asians. All of us were affected by that. And that has then imprinted itself as being something that is just not a piece of real estate. It has an emotional content to it. We are emotionally connected to it, and that is why Hopis are emotionally connected to our landscape, in its entirety. We can articulate that connection to hundreds, if not thousands of points on the landscape. So it is like a spiderweb that is connected to all of these things. And the Hopis are connected to the spiderweb. So we are all interconnected. And we cover this ground up here in our consciousness, in our subconscious, in our culture, in our language. This all personifies itself in our day-to-day thoughts when we think about that landscape."

Gary Paul Nabhan is an ethnobotanist, writer, and adventurer, whose fascination with the Colorado River watershed continues to endure, even after more than thirty years of field research. Gary, along with his wife, Laurie Monti, and I have run the San Juan River in southern Utah and wandered the backcountry of Mexico, where the Sonoran Desert meets the Sea of Cortés. Gary is a champion of those indigenous peoples who continue to seek their tribal destinies within their home habitats.

GARY PAUL NABHAN: "Robert Forbes, who was the first dean of the School of Agriculture at the University of Arizona, took a trip down the Colorado several times in the 1890s and early 1900s, down to the delta. We had this remarkable landscape of what I might call 'watershed agriculture' floodwater-recession agriculture, where people would wait to plant their summer crops after the spring snowmelt increased the flows in the Colorado. And they would go out onto the floodplains' muddy bottoms, sometimes tossing seeds out of their mouth, as well as hand-broadcasting panic grass and other crops unique to the Colorado River system, as well as other ones that had been exchanged over the millennia with Mexican Indian farmers. And that agriculture is uniquely adapted to the Colorado River watershed's heat, salinity, soil fertility, growing-season length, and was absolutely unique in terms of anything else in North America. By 1910 to 1918, we had already lost that system. Aldo Leopold and his brother Carl, one day, canoed down the delta and really saw the remnants of that system. The Cocopah Indian agriculture was already gone and growing back in native and exotic plants. That wonderful mosaic that showed the health of cultural landscapes and natural landscapes interplaying with one another was already lost by the time Aldo Leopold canoed on the delta."

Patty Limerick is a well-known historian, author, and co-founder of the Center of the American West at the University of Colorado in Boulder. Patty's droll humor embellished her description of the mind-set of the eastern Americans when they first entered the arid West of the nineteenth century.

PATTY LIMERICK: "This looked abnormal, deviant, unacceptable, flawed. The language that some people used in the nineteenth century was that it's almost God's error, that He didn't do this right. You'd expect a creator who did such a good job on other areas would be able to carry through. So the irrigation promoters developed the quite wonderful interpretation that this is sort of like a final exam given to humanity, that God is not going to do all the work for you. So you have to take this unfinished project and get the water dammed, kept from dispersing in the spring and early summer, and hold it there so you can green it up. To go through the first round of horror, which I think a lot of people did on the Overland Trail, saying, 'This is the ugliest wasteland. Why would God give us this?' to then get to this next level of cognition of saying, 'Oh, it's a challenge. I get it. Put these parts together, and then you'll have Ohio.'"

In the mid-nineteenth century, a group of Mormons trekked westward and eventually settled near the banks of the Great Salt Lake in northern Utah. Their religious fervor was matched by their relentless industriousness that was vital to their survival in this arid land. As masters of irrigation, they set the tone for future watering of the Southwest. Folklorist and radio producer Hal Cannon is the founding director of the Western Folklife Center in Elko, Nevada. A Utah native, Hal is directly descended from the great Mormon pioneer, Brigham Young.

HAL CANNON: "I grew up with the story of Jim Bridger telling the Mormons that he would give a thousand dollars for the first bushel of corn that was grown in these valleys, coming out of the Wasatch Mountains. The Mormons were proud of all the bushels of corn that they grew out of the wilderness. I remember my dad getting up in the middle of the night to take his turn in irrigation, and just how beautifully organized the irrigation district was, and how, really, the power of the community had a lot to do with your place on the line of irrigation. Oftentimes, the most powerful person in an agricultural community was the water master, in Mormon communities. That is still the case today.

"Lives, as you know, have been lost over water—people taking more than their turn, taking more than their share, people taking advantage of 'high-ority' rather than the fairness of their equal share of water. So I guess I see the power of it on a very small basis. Men out with a plow, or a digger, or shovels and a pick, and making the water go where they wanted it to go. To me, that's the saga of the pioneering experience, not the Corps of Engineers."

The headwaters of the Green and Big Sandy rivers spring from glaciers in the Wind River Range in the Rocky Mountains of Wyoming. This is a landscape where eagles abide and wildlife is abundant. I recall a winter's drive through this country, taking great care as I passed over flat patches of black ice in the roadway where it would be all too easy to lose control of the car. But it was worth every mile to visit a landscape that cradles the Green River watershed. The confluence of the Big Sandy with the Green River occurs several miles north of Rock Springs, Wyoming, home of Western Wyoming Community College. It is here that Charlie Love is a professor of geology. His knowledge of the physical landscape of this area is profound and his intellect is at home at any point in the geologic history of the region.

CHARLIE LOVE: "The reason that those rivers head from that country is due to two kinds of geologic past, one more remote than the other. One is the building of the Rocky Mountains, in what we called the Laramide orogeny, about 70 million years ago, down to about 40 million years ago. The other is the intrusion of Yellowstone National Park. I call it an intrusion because some magnificent hot body of rock down below the continent has been pushed over, and like a blowtorch, it has burned a hole through the continent, and in recent geologic time, the last 2 million years, has exploded three times. Practically on schedule. And this may be one of the reasons the Green River flows the direction that it does."

The headwaters of the Colorado River spring from the western aspect of the Rocky Mountains west of Denver. The main stem of the Colorado River flows southwestward through Colorado, into southeastern Utah, where it is conjoined with the Green and San Juan rivers. The Colorado then flows into Arizona, heading south, separating Arizona from Nevada and California. It passes into Mexico, and finally reaches its delta at the north end of the Sea of Cortés. Traditionally, during the spring the river flooded, burying the floodplains beneath a relentless torrent. In the dry season, the river slowed to a relative trickle. Before construction of the great dams in the twentieth century, agriculturists transplanted from the East envisioned farming the floodplains and irrigating their fields by running water in ditches from the river. But first they had to control the flow of the river.

My good friend the author, historian, and environmentalist William deBuys wrote the text for an award-winning book entitled *Salt Dreams*, with photographs by Joan Meyer. He recounted the story of the extraordinary debacle that resulted in the genesis of the Salton Sea.

WILLIAM DEBUYS: "Essentially, the California Development Company, in the process of developing the burning desert that they rechristened the Imperial Valley, had been having a hell of a lot of trouble getting water to the valley because of the cheap and hurried way they built their main irrigation canal that would bring water from the Colorado River. That first effort at building the canal kept silting up, and so especially when the water was low, as it was in the winter, which was the most crucial growing time in that desert, they couldn't get enough water down the canal to get to the valley. As an expedient, they simply made a shortcut between the bend of the canal and the Colorado River, and just dug an open ditch between those two. They put no headgate in that they could close to shut the flow of water off, if they ever had to. They thought, 'Well, we have got time because the Colorado River won't flood in the wintertime.' Well, sure enough, it flooded in the wintertime, and just burst through this open gap.

"At that time, geologically, the Colorado, having oscillated back and forth across its delta, had been over on the east side of the delta for a long time, and geologically it was time for it to start moving west. Well, here was the great opportunity. An open door, a heavy flow of water, and boom! It went. Essentially, the river adopted the irrigation canal as its main channel, and what then ensued was a kind of apocalyptic experience for the Imperial Valley as the river flooded and flooded and flooded with repeated storms. It followed in the spring again with snowmelt, and for two years, a kind of humpty-dumpty story was played out with all the king's horses and all the king's men trying to put the river back again. They couldn't do it for two years, until finally, with all the resources of the Southern Pacific Railroad, they put together a really crack team of engineers. The gap was finally closed, and the river was constrained within its old channel.

"In the aftermath of this, there was the Salton Sea, created with all this two years of the greater part of the flow of the Colorado River going into the Salton Sink. And this coincided with a new way of thinking about what people in the United States wanted to do about the Colorado River. In a sense, the reverberations of that great flood that filled the Salton Sink shook their way into the creation of the hydraulic society that we have down there today. They led, in a sense, directly—although there were other strains joining this line—to the construction of Boulder, now Hoover Dam, and they led to the Colorado River Aqueduct, and they led to the All-American Canal. They led to the plumbing of the Colorado River."

It had become apparent to agriculturists, developers, politicians, and others that the Colorado River was indeed the aquatic lifeline of the American Southwest. Early on, Southern Californians recognized that these river waters were valuable not only to farmers but also to coastal cities, including Los Angeles and San Diego. It was obvious that the precious waters of the Colorado River would have to be apportioned. I conducted an enlightening interview with attorney William Swan, who is a Colorado River scholar. He addressed many subjects, including the historic meeting held at Bishop's Lodge just north of Santa Fe, New Mexico, that was presided over by then-secretary of commerce Herbert Hoover, which led to the Colorado River Compact of 1922, and the Law of the River.

WILLIAM SWAN: "Congress was appropriating money for diversion works clear back in the 1800s. But when things really got rolling in the late 1800s, early 1900s, there was just simply a huge tension. Because as the West began to develop, you had the populations developing more in the Southwest, in California and along the river in Arizona, and not so much in the other states. And the other states looking at this interstate river said, 'Whoa. Wait a minute. We may be at risk here, because under the doctrine of prior appropriation, somebody who puts the water to use could claim the whole right to the river.' And so they could eventually claim possibly all of the river flow for themselves. So the upper-basin states got very nervous about that and decided to go to Congress. They asked Congress to help with the development of a compact. So Congress consented. They appointed a referee, so to speak, in the form of Mr. Hoover. They sat down and tried to work out a compact. They would like, I think, to have worked out a situation where they could figure out how much each state would get. But that was just too difficult. So they divided it into basins. The upper-basin states of Wyoming, Colorado, Utah, and New Mexico, against the lower-basin states of Arizona, California, and Nevada, tried to work out a division of the water, just to protect each sphere, so to speak. The upper sphere and the lower sphere. And they finally did that by thinking that the river flowed more than 15 million acre-feet a year, and divided it fifty-fifty, 7.5 million acre-feet per year to the upper basin, 7.5 million to the lower basin, as some way of sharing the river in perpetuity so that the upper basin would feel secure.

"In hindsight, it is flawed because the river may not produce that much water, and they recognized at the time that Mexico would eventually need a share of that. Of course, later, in the 1940s, we did work out the treaty with Mexico which gave Mexico a guaranteed 1.5 million [acre-feet]. When you add those up, 7.5, 7.5, and 1.5, you are at 16.5 million acre-feet. And even the Bureau of Reclamation will say the river doesn't produce that every year. It is probably close to 15 million acre-feet, but it is not 16.5. So we will have a crisis someday in the future. So that division under the Colorado River Compact of 1922 is really the foundation of this whole thing."

The dividing line separating the upper basin from the lower basin is located at Lee's Ferry, just south of the state line between Utah and Arizona. Stewart Udall, former Arizona congressman and secretary of the interior, contends that the Colorado River Compact led to events that enabled Californians to develop Colorado River water well in advance of the other six states.

STEWART UDALL: "Herbert Hoover served them well. I have never understood why he was there. He was, in effect, California's agent in putting this through. They wanted an agreement that would enable them to go to Congress and build Boulder [now Hoover] Dam. That was a kind of forced marriage. It ended up with this strange thing, that never happened in other basins, of each state being allocated a certain amount of water. This is purely arbitrary. There was no rational basis for it. Hoover, I am sure, was under pressure. They had to have an agreement that led, of course, to the construction of Boulder Dam. And that enormous project went forward in the depths of the Great Depression. This again showed the political power that Southern California was exerting. And the economic power, because it got the electric power companies involved. This was, in essence, a California project. It wasn't anything beneficial to the basin. And the water flowing down the river to the delta, and flowing to the few irrigation districts like Imperial Valley and other huge users of water—the key water, rather good quality water—was going to Southern California through an aqueduct."

Politicians frequently fall prey to procrastination, especially when they have to ponder considerations beyond the purviews of their constituencies. This may result in faulty legislation that causes profound divisiveness.

In Santa Barbara, I interviewed lifelong Colorado River scholar Norris Hundley, author of *The Great Thirst*, who spoke of major inadequacies of the Colorado River Compact.

NORRIS HUNDLEY: "An important thing to keep in mind about the compact is that it reflects its time in being an ethnocentric document. The Indians weren't invited to participate, nor was there any consideration of giving them a share of the water. Hoover said, 'We don't want to put a wild Indian provision in here, create a problem for ourselves.' Mexico asked to have representation. Prior to this time—it would go on for another two decades—Mexico had been negotiating with the United States over rights to Colorado River water and to water in the Río Grande. The compact negotiator said 'No' to inviting Mexicans. 'We don't want to have the Mexicans here.' Everyone suspected there would someday be a treaty. The basins would share that Mexican burden as they called it. But other than that, nothing was said."

Floyd Dominy served as commissioner of the Bureau of Reclamation during the Eisenhower, Kennedy, and Johnson administrations. Mr. Dominy was witness to the dust bowl years, wherein countless farmers had to pack up and head West, leaving their barren farms whose topsoil was scattered to the winds. These experiences helped shape his thinking and prompted him to focus on initiating myriad irrigation projects that resulted in a major period of dam-building west of the hundredth meridian, that dividing line that separates the verdant eastern United States from the arid West. Many western Americans still shared the mindset that Nature had left the arid West bereft of water, and that it was up to human ingenuity to repair this flaw.

Thus several great diversion projects were created whereby waters were diverted out of the Colorado River watershed into adjacent sparsely watered drainages so that the West could indeed be irrigated. I interviewed Floyd Dominy on his farm in Virginia, where he expressed his reasoning for construction of the most contested dam in America, the Glen Canyon Dam.

FLOYD DOMINY: "Well, you have got to recognize that the Law of the River [defined in the Colorado River Compact] puts the upper basin in a straitjacket. They can't develop their share of the water unless they have control of the river to equalize the flow from wet to dry years, because the law requires them to deliver 7.5 million acre-feet a year, or at least 75 million acre-feet over ten-year moving average. Now that can't possibly done and still leave any water for their development unless they have a huge sponge somewhere, just above the point you measure, so that you can capture the 30 million acre-foot years to balance the 6 million acre-foot years. You never know when that 6 million acre-foot is going to come, and you may have five or six of those years in a row with less than 7.5 million acre-feet of water in the entire year in the Colorado. So this is why Glen Canyon [Dam] is necessary. It had to be located just as close to Lee's Ferry [that divides the upper and lower basins] as possible so you could capture the San Juan, and the Escalante, and the Green, and all the rest of them.

"For example, the city of Albuquerque couldn't depend on its 110,000 acre-feet of water out of the San Juan River, diverted through the channel [the San Juan–Chama diversion], unless it had the storage capacity in Glen Canyon Dam. The water wouldn't be there in many years without Glen Canyon Dam. [This holds for] all of the other diversions in Colorado and Utah and Wyoming where the same thing is true. Glen Canyon Dam is absolutely essential to provide that steady flow of water from the good to the bad years."

Early on, Arizona and California competed for the waters of the Colorado River, a situation that led to what many regard as the greatest water war in the history of the West. In 1963, the Supreme Court awarded Arizona its annual apportionment of 2.8 million acre-feet, as compared with California's 4.4 million acre-feet. However, it was determined that Arizona's apportionment was junior to California's. In other words, during an extended drought, Arizona would have to relinquish a vast proportion of its annual allocation of Colorado River water to California, should there not be enough water to go around. In Las Vegas, Nevada, I met with Patricia Mulroy, the general manager of the Southern Nevada Water Authority and one of the most highly regarded of the so-called "water buffaloes" who manage the waters of the Colorado River.

PATRICIA MULROY: "The state of California probably is the furthest along in looking at water as a commodity. The state of Arizona still has much more of a 'resource perspective,' and it blocks any 'commodity perspective' on water. There is a much closer relationship within the state of Arizona, of the people themselves, to the water supply. People in the state of California don't have a longer-term sense of the water supply, and they are developing along very different lines. Finding bridges there is going to be a real challenge.

"I can appreciate why, when the compacts and the lower-basin arrangements, and *Arizona vs. California*, why all the things happened that did, that led to the state of California claiming a priority water right over the state of Arizona. But step back. This is 2001. Why would a group of cities in California have the right to run water down the streets while the cities in the state of Arizona go dry? That makes no sense. That priority is antiquated. It may have had usefulness between competing economic interests at the agricultural level. But it is preposterous today between cities. So how are you ever going to find common ground in the lower basin, when one state bears the benefit of something happening and the other bears only the consequences? There is a disconnect there. There have to be mutual benefits and mutual consequences. I have long become convinced that unless that cultural view that one state trumping another state saying, 'I have something you don't have' goes away, the problems in the lower basin of the Colorado River are going to be insurmountable."

These problems include not only the over-allocation of the Colorado River that serves a growing human population of more than 25 million but also other King Solomon concerns, such as resolution of prior Indian water rights, the enormous salinity in the Colorado River, pollution from pesticides and nuclear waste, agriculture competing with urbanization and industry, massive evaporation from giant reservoirs, the fact that almost no water now flows from the Colorado River into the delta at the Sea of Cortés, and the effect of the introduction of both the National Environmental Policy Act and the Endangered Species Act on future development within the Colorado River basin and beyond.

Taken together these issues of human provenance comprise a sphere of reference of such complexity that no single mind can encompass it. The inescapable bottom line is that we as a species have exceeded the carrying capacity of the watershed and our collective point of view is dominated by economics. In the last centuries, we have overlain the Colorado River watershed with our ever-growing numbers and our anthropocentric biases. Our presence overwhelms the biotic communities that support and sustain us, yet few heed the consequences of this.

The Colorado River watershed and its myriad human issues provide a highly complex model of what is happening throughout our planet. If those of us with any glimmer of consciousness examine this model and thereafter attempt to extrapolate future probabilities, we'll inevitably if reluctantly realize that we are poised on the edge of a potentially lethal disaster.

Still, I'm guardedly optimistic. I believe there is wisdom yet to be gleaned, and common sense still exists as a course to pursue through the labyrinth of folly that we've wrought. In the subchapters that follow, we'll examine points of view of many whose contributions help round out the conceptual context of human relationship with the flow of Nature.

ii.

When I first gazed into the waters of the Colorado River in 1957, I had no idea how much history I was looking at. I was a youngster hitchhiking across America on Route 66, and I had stopped in Needles, California, to look out over the strange rock formations that gave Needles its name. In 2001, nearly forty-four years later, I took a boat ride on the Colorado River from Needles down through the Topac Gorge to Lake Havasu. Only when our boat cruised the surface of Lake Havasu did I actually see the very point where a pumping station on the west side of the lake pumps billions and billions of gallons of water to Los Angeles and many other cities and communities in Southern California—and a pumping station on the east side where billions of gallons are pumped to Phoenix and Tucson. Without Lake Havasu, the coastal cities of California and the inland desert cities of central Arizona would have developed completely differently—if at all.

A hundred years ago, there was no politically rendered Law of the River that determined how to use the waters of the mighty Colorado. There were no dams and lakes on the river. Author William deBuys addressed the mind-set that prevailed a century ago when the Colorado River still ran wild and farmers needed a reliable source of water.

WILLIAM DEBUYS: "I think that that 1922 meeting up the road here at Bishop's Lodge was held really at the apogee of the ethic that the historian Sam P. Hays has called 'the gospel of efficiency.' This was part of the conservation movement, this idea that, by God, Nature was kind of sloppy. And if we were going to get the land and the waters to support as much of American society as we could, we had to be efficient, and we had to actually improve Nature, and make it more efficient. We were then looking at Nature as though it were simply a machine. The first step to make a machine more efficient was to remove surplus parts, and one of those surplus parts was floods. We had to get rid of those. They were wasteful. Another surplus part was letting fresh water get to the sea.

"We were going to use everything, put everything to work, everything to use, to make the most of this society that we could. And so, the Colorado River Compact of 1922 divided up the waters of the river, and it sort of implicitly told the states, 'By God, you better get on with developing your share because somebody else is really hungrier than you, and that is California. You better get your share and develop it.' The premise was to make that river work, and make every drop in it work for the benefit of society.

"There wasn't the least glimmer of a thought that maybe the river, which makes life possible in this arid country, the river that is the linear oasis along which we live—that the river deserved any of its own water."

Dennis MacBride is a community historian who lives in Boulder City, Nevada. He addressed the relationship between the flooding of the Colorado River, the presence of the Salton Sea, and the construction of Boulder (now Hoover) Dam. Dennis is an authority on the history and lore of the lower Colorado River, and reiterated the story of how the Salton Sea came to be.

DENNIS MACBRIDE: "There was an effort in the early part of the century, in 1904, 1905, 1906, to irrigate the Imperial Valley of California with water from the Colorado River. And they actually dug another channel to try to divert some of the Colorado out into the Imperial Valley, which was a very important agricultural area at the time. Well, unfortunately the river got away from them. And it actually jumped its original bed, original at the time, because it has changed beds many times, and started flowing through the channel that they had dug. And then of course dug a whole new channel right into the Imperial Valley and started filling up the north end of it, which became the Salton Sea. It took them a couple of years to get the river back under control again.

"One of the great motivations for trying to find somewhere to build a dam on the Colorado was to control the flooding, because when it flooded, the river would jump its bank and carve a new channel. So flooding was a terrible problem, and they had to get that under control. One of their ancillary projects was to explore the Colorado River and maybe see where they might build a dam. And there were explorations on the river looking for a dam site into the early 1920s, until they finally narrowed it down to two—Boulder Canyon and Black Canyon. They ultimately changed it from Boulder Canyon, where they were actually going to start building, to Black Canyon."

It would require legislation to divide the waters between the seven states within the Colorado River basin before any dams could be built. As mentioned earlier, Herbert Hoover presided over a meeting in Santa Fe, New Mexico, that resulted in the 1922 Colorado River Compact which divided the river into two basins, the dividing line located at Lee's Ferry. The upper-basin states of Colorado, Wyoming, Utah, and New Mexico apportioned the water among themselves. The lower-basin states of California, Arizona, and Nevada required help from Congress. Arizona refused to sign the compact for two decades. Stewart Udall, a native Arizonan, spoke of the unique the laws that control the flow of the Colorado River.

STEWART UDALL: "The Santa Fe [Colorado River] Compact simply divided waters and produced interstate agreements, although Arizona refused to participate. And they fought it for twenty years because they saw it as California getting the upper hand and dominating the river. They were correct, in my opinion, in that assumption. But they had to have a law, and that became the Boulder Canyon Project, which would spell out what was going to happen if this big dam was built. That was the beginning, really, of what they now call the Law of the River. This was a lawyer's dream. Lawyers in all the affected states had to become acquainted with the law, and then additional laws were written. And now there is a body of law called 'The Law of the River.' This is not true in any other river basin in the United States to this degree. Law governs everything."

Many people who analyze the relative strengths of different states think that California had the most influence, and therefore got the best deal with the 1922 compact. Floyd Dominy disagrees.

FLOYD DOMINY: "As a matter of fact, I am kind of surprised that the compact doesn't favor California more than it does. When you stop and think that the time that compact was drafted in the 1920s, there were fifteen congressmen from California and Arizona and Nevada. There were only eight in the upper-basin states. So the population already favored California. And the influence in Congress already favored California. I'm kind of surprised that it came out the way it did.

"Now, the reason it did was because California wanted Hoover Dam. And they wanted the All-American Canal. They had to have some support from the rest of the West in order to get that. I think, actually, it turned out quite favorably for the upper-basin states."

In 1922, Las Vegas, Nevada, was a tiny community built near springs in the desert. Inasmuch as there was no human population to speak of, Nevada's annual apportionment of 300,000 acre-feet remains very small compared to those of California and Arizona. However, Patricia Mulroy contended that the Colorado River Compact provides a rigid framework within which there is still plenty of room to maneuver.

PATRICIA MULROY: "In my mind, the Law of the River was put into place to prevent any one partner on that river system from being able to get the upper hand on the rest of them. But the Law of the River is flexible enough that it allows states, if in agreement, to do anything they want to do. There are no barriers that are so rigid and so impenetrable that you can't get through them. And they allow common sense and productive partnerships to work."

Water rights attorney William Swan interprets the Law of the River based on his understanding of the history of river development. He reckons that California did very well in Santa Fe in 1922.

WILLIAM SWAN: "The California guys got what they wanted. That is, they got a big dam. They got a controlled river. They got a diversion structure. They got what they wanted. And so the California people got going lickety-split to develop their contracts in 1929. They had to have contracts from the secretary of the interior to use this river water, even if they had developed prior rights. And of course, Congress recognized that some people had already appropriated water, and went to great lengths to protect those prior rights, which they called 'present perfected rights,' on both sides of the river down there [in the lower basin].

"They got these contracts in place among the California users. Who are those users? Imperial Irrigation District, Coachella Valley Water District, Palo Verde Irrigation District, and of course the big giant Metropolitan Water District of Southern California, which [serves Los Angeles and] also eventually served San Diego."

The Reclamation Act of 1902 was intended to help family farmers and ranchers succeed in the arid landscapes of the West. Today, more than 80 percent of California's allocation of Colorado River water goes to agriculture, which is a direct outgrowth of farmers gaining earliest rights to the river. Bruce Babbitt, former secretary of the interior, spoke to me about the original intent of reclaiming the West.

BRUCE BABBITT: "The original philosophy of all of the great big government reclamation projects was sort of an aquatic version of the Homestead Act. The whole idea was to put small people on the land through reclamation. It never really happened in most of the West. I don't think it ever is going to happen. The sort of transition to large-scale agriculture is a fact. It is not what was intended. But it is there, and it is not going to change."

While the intent of the Reclamation Act was to serve small farmers, most people failed to comprehend the ramifications of the fluctuating waters of the Colorado. Folklorist Hal Cannon points out that there is an enormous difference between wet years and dry years, and that the flow of Nature doesn't necessarily coincide with perceived human needs.

HAL CANNON: "If you have lived in a place where you see the effect of the years where there is a lot of water and the years where there is not much water, the difference between those years when tons of water is falling out of the canyons in springtime and those when the snowpack hasn't been very much is so extreme, and the drama between those two amounts is so extreme, that it is hard to believe that you can assume that it is always going to be a constant to just turn on your tap, because Nature doesn't work that way."

How could we know how much water to allocate if we didn't know how much water would flow in any given year? Historian Norris Hundley wrote the book, as they say, on the Colorado River, including one entitled *The Great Thirst*. When I visited him in Santa Barbara, Norris mentioned a serious miscalculation that became a major factor in determining the allocations between the upper and lower basins of the Colorado River.

NORRIS HUNDLEY: "The river-flow assumptions were in error. Some of this became known as early as the 1920s in the debates over the Boulder Canyon Project. There was a Colorado River Board created for that project. And the folks there went out, consulted some of the more recent measurements, and felt that there was nowhere near 17 or 18 million [acre-feet of annual flow]. Maybe 15 million acre-feet. Additional measurements were made, and finally they determined that based on the evidence they had, there would be no more than about 14 million acre-feet in the river, at best, on an average. Remember, their basic allocation was 16 million acre-feet. A million and a half went to Mexico as a priority. Mexico's right was vested in a treaty. And a treaty has all the clout of the Constitution. You can't violate a treaty without probably going to war with Congress and Mexico eventually. It has first priority.

"But like most new knowledge that you don't want to hear, that you don't want to believe, it took a long time for this shock to make itself really felt. So many of the people in the [lower] basin were in shock. Many still believe that the upper basin would never use its full allocation. Somehow, science would bail them out."

Jim Nafsey is an engineer employed by the Metropolitan Water District that serves the coastal cities of California. Jim is also a history buff, and provided a fascinating glimpse into the mind-set that led to construction of both Hoover Dam that resulted in Lake Mead and Parker Dam that resulted in Lake Havasu.

JIM NAFSEY: "In the early 1900s, we had this wild, untamable river that didn't have any dams on it. In the springtime, when we had the snowmelt, it would wash out farms, crops, cattle, anything that got in its way. And in drought situations, there were places you could walk across the river. And we had these thousands of men come into the area and actually start building two major dam projects on the river that were pretty much being built concurrently. The first, as we know, was the Boulder [now Hoover] Dam. And the second one was little old Parker Dam of which the Metropolitan Water District actually sponsored about 95 percent of the cost to construct. And this dam's purpose was to create a full bay of water to pump from for the Colorado River Aqueduct. Now when we look back, we couldn't pump from this river that would run raging in the springtime and almost dry out in the wintertime. So we needed to dam that water up to have a full bay of water to pump from."

The Colorado River Aqueduct extends from the western bank of Lake Havasu westward to near Los Angeles, and then segues into the San Diego aqueducts that transport much of the water that serves San Diego. Other water is transported to Los Angeles and beyond by the California Aqueduct, which is fed mainly by rivers in northern California. In reality, the coastal cities of California rely precariously on Nature's whims for their water, and all too few of the residents have any real sense of the complex plumbing system that occurs immediately upstream from their faucets, showerheads, and commodes.

Dennis MacBride recounted lore that he had gathered about some of the movers and shakers, whose perseverance resulted in construction of both Hoover and Parker dams.

DENNIS MACBRIDE: "Frank Crowe probably is the one most responsible for bringing the Six Companies together, the constituent companies into the organization called Six Companies, which built the [Hoover] dam. But he was up and down the Colorado River as early as the early part of the twentieth century. And he always said, and I have this from people I interviewed who knew him and whose parents knew him, that he 'was going to build a dam on the Colorado River.' So he was involved over two, almost three decades before they started construction on the dam. And over those years—say 1902 when the Reclamation Service was founded, up to 1928 when they signed the Boulder Canyon Project Act, when Coolidge approved it—Crowe gathered kind of a core group of construction workers that followed him from job to job, and ultimately followed him out here to Hoover Dam."

Parker Dam resulted in Lake Havasu, the reservoir from which water is now pumped by the Metropolitan Water District to the coastal cities of California.

Jim Nafsey recounts a story from the days of the dam's construction that reveals the intensity of the rivalry between Arizona and California to control the river.

JIM NAFSEY: "You know, back in 1934, I think it was, Arizona didn't want any part of the Parker Dam. In fact, Governor Moore at the time decided that he was not going to let any Californians tell him what to do. He decided to send out about half a dozen National Guardsmen to stop the Metropolitan Water District from the construction of the Parker Dam.

"So they came over to Parker, Arizona, from Phoenix, and met up with Nelly Bush in Parker. And they got on the *Julia B.*, which was one of Nelly's ferryboats that she ran up and down the river. And she brought them up the river as far as she could, as close as she could to the construction site for the Parker Dam, and let these National Guardsmen off. They had a three-day trek up to what is called Take Off Point, where they actually set up camp. And they were going to stop the surveyors for the Metropolitan Water District from rowing across the river and doing the survey work required to lay out for the Parker Dam.

"Well, little did they [the National Guardsmen] know as they went through the hot summers, where temperatures get up to 128 degrees, that they couldn't find any water to drink. They thought they could actually drink the water from the river, this muddy brown river that people used to say, 'This river is too thick to drink and too thin to plow.' It would take over two days for it to settle out a glass of water so you can get a little bit of water to drink. And these poor guys are out there in the heat, they didn't have enough water, didn't have enough food. The surveyors from Metropolitan [Water District] actually felt sorry for them so they would give them food and sandwiches and water. And they would be rowing across the river and 'Hey guys, how you doin'?' and having a good time. Got to know each other fairly well.

"One day, Governor Moore really decided that it was time to stop the Metropolitan Water District, so he really came down on the National Guardsmen. They were building up the troops by then. I think at one time, they had almost a hundred National Guardsmen.

"So one day, as the story goes, they are rowing across the river, and the surveyors pop up from their side. And the National Guardsmen pop up from their side of the river. And they fire a couple of shots across the surveyors' riverboat. 'You Californians get on back to your side! Us Arizonans don't need any part of that dam, and you are not going to tell us what to do!'

"Well, that actually started one of the longest legal battles in the history of the United States—*Arizona vs. California*. And it was all over water rights. And to this day, really, water rights are still key to growth of communities. But it really is a required commodity for growth and for the health of all communities. So a reliable source of water is imperative. And that is what the Metropolitan Water District is most concerned with is to be a reliable source of water to the coastal plains of Southern California."

Dennis MacBride: "The men who came to work as high scaleman, they had no experience. They were just men who were hungry enough that they would hang 700 feet above the bottom of the canyon on a little bosun's chair tied to a steel [pole] knocked in the ground, another 100 feet above them on a rope. And they swung back and forth. They became very agile of course, through experience, in swinging out from here to there, and prying the rock off, and drilling the holes for blasting and so on. But, you know, it didn't actually take any particular skill. Just the ability not to have acrophobia, and the ability to hang on to this rope.

"One gentleman that I interviewed was Joe Kine, who actually has a monument now raised to him, down at the dam. They dragged a big rock down there to the visitor's center, and a local artist made a larger than life sized bronze of Joe Kine, the high scaler. Joe said it was the best job on the project, because it was a sitting-down job. Yeah, there is one very famous story. It is well known, where someone had fallen off the cliffs, and one of the high scalers swung out on his rope and caught this man before he plunged all the way down to the bottom and died. The high scaler himself, who swung out, actually got an award from some company that manufactured watches, so he became their endorsement. And that story also found its way into Zane Grey's novel about construction of the dam called *Boulder Dam*."

Floyd Dominy: "I saw Hoover Dam for the first time on January 2, 1937. And I marveled that any outfit could have the know-how and the vision to construct something like that. It just was a magnificent thing, as big as the pyramids, as beautiful as the Taj Mahal. But these of course were monuments to the dead. The Hoover Dam was a monument to the living."

I've toured Hoover Dam, and I agree with Floyd Dominy that it is indeed one of the great engineering marvels of all time. At the time of my visit, Gary Bryant was responsible for the day-to-day management of the Hoover Dam. He gave me an idea of the magnitude of the structure.

GARY BRYANT: "If you look at the dam, it is kind of deceiving, but at the base of the part down by bedrock, probably from the top to the bottom, it is about 700 feet. But it is also that wide at the bottom. It is almost as wide as it is tall. Now when you look at it at the top, it is only 45 feet wide. But it goes down into this triangular pattern. So it is really quite wide. The water backed up right behind the dam is about 500 feet deep. So it is quite a deep dam, and quite a deep reservoir."

It wasn't until 1944 that the United States actually began to work out a treaty with Mexico regarding their allocation of water from the Colorado River. Stewart Udall was serving in the United States Army Air Corps at the time.

STEWART UDALL: "The history of the 1944 treaty with Mexico was during the war, 1944, and obviously was an effort by President Roosevelt to mollify the Mexican officials. They had agriculture south of the Imperial Valley. And Baja, California, was a rich agricultural area, and they wanted to protect their water. And they said, 'You divided up the river, but you left us out.' And so this treaty guaranteed Mexico a certain amount of water. And that was the 1944 U.S.–Mexico Treaty. It wasn't a treaty with the states. It was the United States of America and the government of Mexico."

Bruce Babbitt reminded me that water and power generation are intertwined. Indeed, many of the great dams generate enormous amounts of hydroelectric power and thus serve dual functions of creating storage reservoirs and lighting up the landscape.

BRUCE BABBITT: "The building of dams never really was a very big enterprise until Thomas Edison came along and invented uses for electricity. That just set off a cataract of demand because people began to understand that hydroelectric power, then really the principle source of power, was very valuable. It just set off a rush of dam building because dams were viewed as cash registers. Build a dam and you get a cascade of money coming out of them with the electrical generators. And I suspect, more than anything, it was the demand for hydropower that led to this lamentable kind of dam on every river in the West. But now what is happening is the curves are crossing. Because when they first started building dams, water was valuable but not nearly as much in demand as electricity. Those curves are going to cross in the days coming when the water will be vastly more valuable than the electricity it generates. And those dams won't look nearly as interesting because of all the tremendous losses through evaporation from the reservoirs."

Historian Patty Limerick addressed the history of the Department of the Interior, and the enormous responsibility that is delegated through its various bureaus, as well as interdepartmental competition for bureaucratic control of the American landscape.

PATTY LIMERICK: "The Department of the Interior was formed in 1849 as a real recognition that the United States was an empire. The United States was cast with a self-image, we were the colony that revolted against the empire, and now we are independent. But by 1849 it was perfectly clear that the United States had a continuous land empire.

"You can't have an empire casually. Empire is not something that you would tend to every few years. You really do have to rule an empire. So, Interior really represents that. And then, as the conservation movement gets going, and as new designations of lands and permanent public ownership come in, that moves into sort of the home office for ruling that western empire. So all the agencies—the Bureau of Indian Affairs, the Bureau of Reclamation, National Park Service, an agency that began as the grazing service, then became the Bureau of Land Management. Anomalously the National Forest Service and [the Department of] Agriculture were not Interior. Harold Ickes in the 1930s was still trying really hard to get the Forest Service back over to Interior. So it turns out that there is this really remarkable consolidated power over western destinies in this thing called the Department of the Interior."

In 2001, Laurie Gray was assistant director for the lower Colorado region of the Bureau of Reclamation. When I visited her in her Boulder City office, she provided some perspective regarding the role of the Bureau of Reclamation in managing the waters in the lower Colorado.

LAURIE GRAY: "Primarily in the lower Colorado region from Lee's Ferry down to the Mexican border, we manage the river on behalf of the secretary of the interior. The secretary has been deemed the water master through a Supreme Court ruling, and so, we manage the river after contracts, paying attention to who is using what amount of water. We try to provide habitat for species that will allow us to continue to manage the river. And then we have some facilities on the river, Hoover Dam, Davis Dam, Parker Dam. And we actually manage those three facilities, which are all hydroelectric power-producing facilities."

BRUCE BABBITT: "When the environmental movement in this country really grew up at the turn of the twentieth century . . . they were looking at the land in the forest. The water kind of escaped their attention. And remarkably enough, the interest in water in its ecological function on the landscape never really got moving until the 1960s, '70s, and '80s. And the difficulty is that by the end of the twentieth century, these water-development projects had no ecological analysis or complement to them at all. So when Glen Canyon Dam was built, nobody even asked the questions, 'What will this do downstream to the Colorado River in terms of the native fish species, in terms of the beaches along the Grand Canyon?' For whatever reason, we were very late coming to the issue of water and how it sustains and nourishes the creation and the beauty and diversity of the landscape."

iii.

As mentioned earlier, the Colorado River system drains an area of about 244,000 square miles, or almost one-twelfth the land area of the coterminous United States.

When the Colorado River Compact of 1922 was enacted, the population of the watershed was considerably smaller, and many who lived here were both traditional Native Americans and relatively new ranch and farm families who subsisted through their own hard work. However, during the twentieth century there was phenomenal growth in urban centers, including Los Angeles, San Diego, Phoenix, Tucson, Denver, Salt Lake City, Albuquerque, and scores of other communities. Now the urban population far exceeds that of the rural. These rural and indigenous peoples who are clinging to their traditional ways of life now share characteristics with endangered species. The upper-basin states of the Colorado River system include Wyoming, Colorado, Utah, and New Mexico. California, Arizona, and Nevada are in the lower basin. For years, California has been using far more water than that to which it is entitled. This so-called borrowed water has gone unused in the upper basin. Presently the people in the upper basin are concerned that their way of life is threatened if they continue to forfeit their water. As I visited their communities and remote ranches, they spoke to me of their history and of the desire of upstream communities to preserve their cultural traditions through the coming generations.

Anne Zwinger is a writer, naturalist, and river runner who has honed her own consciousness by observing and writing about what she sees in the wild. She has visited the headwaters of the main rivers in the Colorado River watershed.

ANNE ZWINGER: "It was wonderful to stand on a glacier and listen to the click-ing-dripping sound of water melting, and knowing that was the Green River. And of course, pellucid cold running at thirty-two degrees, very different from the way it is at the confluence where it is gritty and muddy and swirling, and a dif-ferent river that has worked through its landscape. It is the same business as see-ing the place in the mountains change. It was thought-provoking to start at one end and see it end at the other. And of course, I think it really ends in the Sea of Cortés."

Trapping, mining, ranching, and farming have been sustained by the Col-orado River in the upper-basin states. John Beech is a lore master who lives in Rock Springs, Wyoming. John invited me to his home, and told me something about mountain men who financed their adventures by trapping and hunting wild game throughout the intermountain west early in the nineteenth century.

JOHN BEECH: "They were called mountain men because of course they lived pri-marily in the mountains. They were the explorers. They were the people that found all the stuff that was out here. Many of the rivers, streams, are named after these trappers, or mountain men. They ranged throughout the Rocky Mountain West."

Mormons began to settle Utah in the mid-nineteenth century. Joe Benion is a Utah native, whose ancestry goes back to the early Mormon pioneer days. He tells the story of an old mountain man challenging Brigham Young to make the land productive.

JOE BENION: "You know, when Brigham Young surveyed this area, he wanted to spread out the people to get them out over this land, and get it colonized, and build this kingdom in the desert. The mind-set of those early Mormon leaders was that we were here to establish God's Zion in the wilderness, make this desert blossom as a rose. Jim Bridger, the trapper, said to Brigham Young, 'If you can grow a bushel of corn in that Great Basin, I'll give you a thousand dollars.' It was considered a complete wasteland, good for coyotes, rattlesnakes, and goshutes.

"So here we came. And my people [ancestors] were in the second wagon train in October of 1847. Right away, they started establishing this network throughout the desert. And of course, water was where you could establish a community. For the whole south and east portion of this region, you are looking at the watershed of the Colorado River. These little communities started around where there was a river available. And the principle function of Mormons, it seemed to be at that time, was to divert water out of its course and onto fields."

The Little Snake River is part of the Colorado River system. The communities of Baggs and Savory lie just north of the state line between Wyoming and Colorado. This is presently ranching country where wildlife still abounds, and the habitat gives the appearance of good health despite the period of drought that has befallen much of the American West in the opening years of the twenty-first century. The life of Donna Connor has been largely shaped by this habitat and its human history, which is full of outlaw lore.

DONNA CONNOR: "That is what we're famous for—Butch Cassidy and the gang. And they did come to Baggs. It's always been this little out-of-the-way place, where it's safe. And it was safe for them. They had supporters in the community. When they came to this little town, they were 'good citizens.' They did not abuse or disturb, or anything. They used it as a rest place and a haven. And then farther along on the Little Snake River, down in Powder Wash country, which is supposed to have had a hideout, and I believe it, because I have been down. It would be a perfect place for it. Yeah. Old Tom Vernon had the hotel and all the old buildings in Baggs for years and years. And he was a friend of Butch's. He befriended him when he came to town. And he always swore until his death, that Butch did come back from South America, and came through and said hello."

Donna Connor is godmother to the daughter of Mr. and Mrs. Patrick O'Toole, who run a cattle-and-sheep ranch in the Little Snake River country. Patrick O'Toole is extremely mindful of the health of the landscape, and is a primary strategist among sheep ranchers, especially as it concerns marketing. He told me about ranching in Wyoming as we sat in the cab of his pickup truck looking out over the landscape that he stewards.

PATRICK O'TOOLE: "This country here in the desert is 6,500 to 8,500 feet [above sea level]. It is sagebrush, and crested wheatgrasses, and Indian rice grasses, and salt sage. We rotate this country so that in the summertime, this lower part of this desert doesn't get grazed at all. And we come back here in November and do our grazing then. Our upper country is very much Basque country.

"Our forest permits start the fifteenth of June to the first of July, and then we graze on the forest until around the first of October, depending on the specific allotment. It is tremendous cow country, and tremendous sheep country. In my mind, there is a philosophy of how you do things that includes how well the land does. We have fellows, people from the Little Snake River valley, show up at a national meeting, and they talk about how you do things right. We think we understand water, and we understand the land. This is one of the last places that really is still an agricultural valley.

"As you travel around the West, it is very disheartening to me to see what has happened to a lot of communities. When you drop from the Little Snake River drainage to the Elk River drainage, it is trophy homes and subdivisions, and moving fast in that direction. It's a heartbreaker. It's a generational destruction of these open spaces. I haven't mentioned the elk and the deer and the antelope, and all of the other game that is in this area. But this is a tremendously bountiful productive area. We would like to figure out some way to keep it somewhat like it is now."

As the eagle flies, the community of Pinedale, Wyoming, lies less than twenty miles west of the Continental Divide near the western base of the Wind River Range that boasts peaks of more than 13,000 feet above sea level. The headwaters of the Green River spring forth nearby, and the human population of this countryside is still sparse. Echoes of nomadic Indians ring in the wind, and ghosts of mountain men still haunt this habitat of clear air and big sky.

I passed through Pinedale and stopped to meet the mayor of the town, a spirited lady named Rose Skinner, who gave me a point of view shared by many of her neighbors.

ROSE SKINNER: "I was born in Pavillion, Wyoming, which is a little town across the mountains. I was born there because my dad and mom had a ranch, and Mom had to get as close to a doctor as she could because I was born in May and the weather was bad. And on this small ranch we had a reservoir. Our water rights were in that reservoir. And when I was growing up, that was my first idea of what water rights meant, because they were arguing then over how much water my dad could put on his land, because he stopped up this creek, that part of it that goes on down. Water rights have always been a very high priority, and a worrisome subject in Wyoming."

As mentioned earlier, the upper-basin states of Wyoming, Utah, Colorado, and New Mexico are obliged by the Colorado River Compact of 1922 to ensure that the lower-basin states of Arizona, Nevada, and California receive the annual collective apportionment of 7.5 million acre-feet of water. The rural residents of the upper-basin states are clearly aware that the presence of water relies on the flow of Nature, and that the arid Southwest is the site of cycles of drought that can be readily documented through dendrochronology, the science of tree-ring dating. When the snowpack in the mountains is light, less water flows throughout the watershed and there is less water to share with the lower-basin states in spite of the Law of the River.

Rural people who live handcrafted lives are by necessity tuned into the flow of Nature. The difference in perspective between rural Americans and megalopolitan Americans is enormous. In a sense, the upper basin flows through a time warp, while the lower basin is caught in a speed trap. This is not to say that every human living in the upper basin is a model of ecological enlightenment.

The dark truth that lies at the heart of our current economic paradigm is that the commodification of Nature's yield, of turning habitat into money for the sake of money, results in a spiritual dissociation from our planet, thereby disallowing our intuitive understanding of our relationship to our mother vessel. And thus we perch on the edge of having bankrupted Earth's capacity to support us. At our current rate of consumption, we have exceeded the carrying capacity of the Colorado River watershed, itself a model of what has come to prevail around the planet.

C. L. "Chip" Rawlins is a fine writer whose works include *Broken Country* and *Sky's Witness*. He lives outside of Laramie, Wyoming. I visited Chip in his home, and he shared his thoughts about the ability of ranchers to hold on to their water rights in the future.

CHIP RAWLINS: "The water law of the West, and the structure of which states get what, in large part was crafted to facilitate the development of all these irrigated farms that were supposed to spring up. The need for the water is obviously greater in the lower basin. There are more people there. There is a lot more development, more industry than in the upper-basin states like Wyoming. So there is a lot of legal machinery in place that keeps people, individuals in Wyoming who own rights, from selling those rights, for instance, to the Los Angeles Water Department, or whatever they call it [Metropolitan Water District]. That structured law that keeps the water in the basins like that has been pretty resistant to change.

"[Some] of these wealthy characters, a lot of whom are buying ranchland in the upper Green River, have the brains to realize that they are not going to make any money on cows. It is probably a good tax write-off. And aside from having their own private barony with their little helicopter pad next to their house, as many of them do, I think that the other attraction for them is purely financial. I think they can probably see a time in ten years or so when the demand for water in the lower basin is going to be so great that these legal structures that keep people in states like Wyoming from directly selling water rights downstream—these structures are going to be under a lot of assault. Financially, legally, as the agricultural people lose their economic clout, which they are increasingly doing, they are going to lose a lot of this iron-fisted control over water law and water rights. I think that some people who are more oriented toward profit are going to see an opportunity in transferring rights downstream and making a hell of a lot of money without really turning a finger. So in other words, having a flood irrigation right on an upper Green River cattle ranch flood your 'grass-pay' meadow could make you a lot more money if that water goes downstream and ends up in swimming pools in Los Angeles."

Professor Charlie Love at Western Wyoming Community College in Rock Springs has a finely honed ecological orientation. He is a master of what Garrett Hardin defined as "ecolate thinking," the ability to review a system of factors and subsequently extrapolate future probabilities. Here he relates how quickly we can negatively affect the land through irrigation.

CHARLIE LOVE: "You can see down near Manila, Utah, right now, the alkali because of irrigation coming out of the soils in less than one hundred years of irrigation. Ours has gotten much more alkaline, mostly in the form of gypsum. And because of irrigation, you sink it down, and it comes back up and evaporates up, and it draws the alkali with it, and leaves it as a white crust on the surface. It happens naturally, but you accelerate the process with irrigation. The classic place to me is right over the South Pass around Lander. In late summer, the alkali is so fierce that you can't even get a Russian thistle to grow there. And they don't have any pasturage that is unaffected by their irrigation in an increasing alkaline way. It is visible.

"In fact, I use this, and have used it for ten years, as an example to my geology field students, as we go out every year across this. I say, 'Take a look at this. This is what we have done in a hundred years. How much bigger an area do you think they'll be in the next hundred years.' The same thing is happening at Farson with trona as sodium bicarbonate that is coming out on the surface. It is ferocious stuff. It doesn't take long to ruin farmland."

Administration and management of the upper Colorado River falls within the purview of the Bureau of Reclamation. I visited then–deputy director Rick Gold in his office in Salt Lake City, who referred to the Upper Basin Compact of

1948. This compact defines the agreement between the upper-basin states of Colorado, Wyoming, Utah, and New Mexico as to their respective annual allocations of Colorado River water. He went on to describe the Colorado River Storage Project Act of 1956 (CRSP) that was designed to help farmers and ranchers have access to water for agriculture for very low cost, and subsequently resulted in construction of a series of dams that could generate hydroelectric power.

RICK GOLD: "CRSP yielded a plan for a storage project that is actually an amalgam of several mainstream units, as they are called, Glen Canyon [Dam] being one of those. Aspinall Unit [Dam] being another, and three dams over in Colorado that include the Navajo Unit [Dam] and the Flaming Gorge Unit [Dam]. Those are called the mainstream or the initial units of the Colorado River Storage Project. [There are] about twenty-one other associated projects called the 'participating' projects. And those projects are called participators because they participate through the funding mechanism of power revenues, helping to repay the irrigation aid for irrigation in the upper basin. Those mainstream units, all except Navajo [Dam], in CRSP have federal hydropower. And that hydropower generates power at cost and is sold to the public power utilities across the West. The revenue that comes from the sale of that hydropower generation then not only pays for the investment in hydropower, but it pays for that portion of the irrigation investment that is beyond the individual irrigators' ability to repay. And that is sort of the background of what and why the Colorado River Storage Project came to being. It was an upper basin–wide plan for the development of the Colorado River, through storage, initial units, and through participating projects."

In other words, CRSP resulted in construction of myriad hydroelectric dams throughout the upper Colorado River watershed to result in both creation of upstream reservoirs and generation of a vast amount of hydroelectric power that could be sold through electrical utilities companies throughout the West. It could also be provided to agriculturalists for pumping irrigation water from the watercourses and reservoirs. Because of the prevailing anthropocentric notion of the "gospel of efficiency," little or no regard for ecological balance was factored into anyone's thinking, at least at the outset.

Colorado contributes a large proportion of water to the Colorado River. Denver lies east of the Rocky Mountains, outside the Colorado River basin. In order to get water to Denver's burgeoning population, diversion tunnels were constructed that extend from the Frasier and Blue rivers, both tributaries of the

Colorado, to the eastern slope of the Rockies. I visited with Chips Barry, then-director of the Denver Water Board. Chips revealed a concern he has about how the state of Colorado and other upper-basin states jeopardize their water rights if they don't use them.

CHIPS BERRY: "The biggest issue that is there between upper and lower basins is whether the upper basin could sell or lease their 'excess water' to somebody in the lower basin. And if so, is that a wise thing to do? Utah and Colorado have different views on that, generally speaking. Utah, I think, sometimes would like to do that. Colorado thinks that that would undercut the protection afforded to the state by the [upper basin] interstate compact of 1948. You turn water into a commodity, as opposed to something protected by the compact, you are going to lose the protection. Essentially, what the Colorado River Compact of 1922 does is protect states from the operation of their own internal mechanism, which is use it or lose it. If you don't use it, eventually you lose it.

"The 1922 Colorado River Compact set up, essentially, a protection against the application of that [use it or lose it] doctrine between the states. There is no rule that Colorado has to use our apportionment or we lose it to California. California can use it when we don't use it, but they don't obtain a right to it. The fear is if you end up trading that water away, you may lose that protection. And I think that is a valid theory."

American culture is the beneficiary of the ancestral European proclivity for establishing geopolitical boundaries and attendant governing bureaucracies that have thus overlain the continental mosaic of bioregions with state lines and other boundaries that have little to do with Nature's arrangement of natural ecosystems and watersheds.

Historian and author Patty Limerick is possessed of a unique mind that relentlessly penetrates to the heart of the matter.

PATTY LIMERICK: "We do have these state borders now, and they are hilarious, really. If they weren't consequential, they would be very funny. The notion of straight lines—a Lewis Carroll kind of a moment. The idea of putting these big blocks out there and calling them meaningful is really quite a magnificent act of human goofiness. And then it turns out to be quite consequential, so the hilarity dies down pretty fast. But it is a remarkably incompatible set of arrangements that you would have these units of shared concerns and shared destinies and people [complicated] by the weirdness of where the straight line comes through and sets them apart from each other, and forces them to lobby for funds against each other, and contest each other in ways that are not really very sensible."

Most of the human population of Utah lives west of the Wasatch Mountains, and therefore west of the Colorado River basin. The ongoing Central Utah Project is designed to pump water westward out of the basin to serve the 2 million people who live along the Wasatch front in Salt Lake City and other cities and towns in central Utah. This is but one of several examples of water being relocated from one watershed to another to serve human needs.

Well to the southeast of Salt Lake City is the community of Moab, Utah, near where the Green and Colorado rivers conjoin. In the mid-twentieth century, this region provided much of America's uranium that went into the production of atomic bombs. The residue of uranium mining is still gathered in an enormous nuclear tailing site near the banks of the Colorado River close to Moab, and remains yet another important area of jeopardy. This site has been contaminating the river since the 1950s. Bill Heddon is a Harvard-trained scientist who lives near the Colorado River and has grave concerns about the Atlas uranium tailing site.

BILL HEDDON: "Altogether they accumulated 13 million tons of uranium tailings there, fine toothpaste-like material that is laced with radioactivity, and ammonia, and salts, and heavy metals, in an unlined bathtub that was dug in the floodplain of the river. It became the fifth-largest uranium tailings pile in the United States, and the largest one located anywhere near a river. The river at that point breaks out of its banks and runs across that level floodplain any time that the flow exceeds about 45,000 [cubic] feet per second in the spring. We have measurements that go back to 1913 that show it happened twenty-three times in the last century. On average, almost once every four years, you had the river flooding up to the base of the tailings pile. We have been waiting for another year where that 13 million tons of mill waste will be sitting in the river. The tailings are radioactive enough that they can make the water legally unfit to drink. And that water is the drinking water for 25 million Americans downstream. In Southern California, 16 million people get water from the Metropolitan Water District. Two hundred and three cities, I think, get their water from the river, including San Diego, Las Vegas, the Central Arizona Project carrying it down to Phoenix, and parts of Tucson. It is really a pretty critically important resource that we are playing with."

In northwestern New Mexico, I visited my elderly friend Sarah Natani, a Navajo weaver and sheepherder who lives near Shiprock, and who spent time on her uncle's farm beside the San Juan River when she was a child. The San Juan is a tributary of the Colorado River.

SARAH NATANI: "Well, my uncle, his name was Ben Totah, and he used to have a farm over there. There was a big ditch there. And then I guess they used to pump the water through there. And then we used to get a bucket of water there, and drink water from it. And none of us ever got sick from drinking that San Juan River. And I know that water is very precious to everybody. Not only to Navajos, or White Man, or anybody. The Great Spirit has put the water there for us to all share it, to use it. Not one person takes over the whole water."

Much of New Mexico's apportionment goes to the Navajo Indian Irrigation Project near Farmington, where the Navajo Nation administers one of the largest corporate farms in America. This irrigation project was originally intended to provide water for individual small Navajo farms. But as time passed, the Navajos opted to pursue a much larger tribal enterprise. I met with Walter Krakow, director of the Navajo Indian Irrigation Project. For a whole day, we cruised the back roads and visited many sites within the project. He described how in return for funding and constructing the irrigation project, the Navajos would allow part of their water to be diverted out of the San Juan River watershed and into the Río Grande watershed to ensure that Albuquerque and environs would have a stable water supply. This is known as the San Juan–Chama diversion.

WALTER KRAKOW: "In the 1950s there was this desire by the state of New Mexico to build the San Juan–Chama diversion and to deliver water from what they believed was the water-rich San Juan River basin into the Río Grande basin. At that time they believed, and we believe it today as well, that the Navajo Nation had primary rights to the water on the San Juan River, that they were the senior water-rights holders. They had a Winters Doctrine right to the water as well. The state of New Mexico and the federal government began to negotiate with the Navajo Nation about taking a piece of that Winters right water and moving that water through a diversion into the Río Grande basin. They struck a deal, moving 110,000 acre-feet of water on an annual basis, on the average, into the Río Grande valley in exchange for the Navajo Indian Irrigation Project [NIIP] being built. In 1962, in the same piece of legislation, both the San Juan–Chama [Diversion] project and the Navajo Indian Irrigation Project were authorized. We became sort of sister projects. The San Juan–Chama project was built on time, on budget and began to deliver water into the Río Grande basin in 1979. On the NIIP project, we're just a little behind, still not complete. We are only about 60 percent complete on the NIIP project."

Stewart Udall provided a historic sketch of the Winters Doctrine which is vital to the preservation of Indian water rights.

STEWART UDALL: "As a result of the Reclamation Act [of 1902], which was a broad act covering the West, you immediately encountered Indian water rights. In a case in Montana, the Supreme Court handed down what is called the Winters Doctrine [in 1908] that said in effect that when Indian reservations were created, that the law assumed that they would have sufficient water for whatever needs they had, then or in the future, in their little river basin or river system. That of course was a godsend to Indians. Not much was done to implement it, but it has been there. And that doctrine was, I can tell you, in the 1960s when I was there [as secretary of the interior], we saw it as giving us authority to the man that Indian water rights be defined and protected and that Indian projects be pushed forward. We didn't do enough. But that one lawsuit is in many ways more important than the Law of the River."

Stewart served as both U.S. congressman from Arizona and as secretary of the interior during some of these negotiations. He has always been an ardent supporter of Indian water rights, and has a long and honorable history of defending Native American's rights to land, water, and cultural destiny. He is also aware of the genesis of transporting water out of the Colorado River basin.

STEWART UDALL: "Southern California had pioneered it by taking water out of one basin and putting it into another. So the San Juan–Chama project, it is not large, but they are taking water from the Colorado River basin system and putting it in the Río Grande basin system. And Albuquerque and Santa Fe, and the other communities now, are talking about tapping the river [Río Grande] for this water. It also forced New Mexico to recognize Navajo Indian water rights to a degree and build a project for them. And Senator [Clinton] Anderson from New Mexico was a powerful chairman of the committee, pushed this through. I don't know what he was thinking about, but I was thinking, 'Gee, that is going to be a good thing because it will provide family farms for thousands of Navajo Indians, who could become irrigation agriculturists.'"

We live in a time of accelerated change. Passing from the rural countryside to the urban centers of the American Southwest it is like hopping back and forth between the nineteenth and twenty-first centuries. Everyone drinks water from the same water systems, but our values don't always coincide. Rancher Patrick O'Toole expresses his heartfelt belief in rural values.

PATRICK O'TOOLE: "You know, when you go to a rural community basketball game or a picnic, or whatever it is that we do during the year to get together, you see people and you know that they work hard every day. And you know that they have beliefs about their Maker, and about the land. And we are losing that. [Thomas] Jefferson would be rolling over in his grave if he knew what directions we were trying to take this country right now, because we don't have an overall rural policy. America has really weathered the telecommunications issues, or whether it be electrical distribution issues, or water distributions issues. America lately has been very willing to sacrifice rural people for other needs. And when you do that, you lose more than the land. You lose more than the traditions here. You lose the next generation of kids. And I feel very strongly that there is something rural kids and rural populations give America that it can never generate anywhere else. So it is a question of work ethic and the ability to deal with crisis, and the ability to improvise when the time is there. And these kinds of kids are not replaceable. The reality is, rural America produces something very special for America. And we have to be cognizant of that when we start making these policies, especially at a time of limits."

iv.

The mid-twentieth century was a time of great clashes and contentions over the Colorado River. As mentioned earlier, the competition for water between California and Arizona was fierce. Gradually I've come to understand something of the intricate balance between water and electricity in the West. Indeed, the presence of water in desert country inevitably leads to urban growth, and modern cities require electricity. Many of the dams constructed throughout the Colorado River system generate hydroelectricity to supply power to irrigation projects as well as to communities and cities throughout the West. The truth is that the 25 million of us who live in and around the Colorado River watershed are connected by the water that the river yields as well as by the electricity that it generates. The water and hydroelectric power generated by the Colorado River helped jump-start the behemoth of California, which is now one of the ten greatest economies in the world.

Stewart Udall was born in St. Johns, Arizona, in 1920. He was elected to the United States Congress in 1952, and in 1961, President John F. Kennedy appointed him as secretary of the interior, where he remained for eight crucial years. Stewart once told me that originally he was of the Teddy Roosevelt school of conservation. His thinking evolved during his years with the Department of the Interior as he was forced to balance his natural environmental inclinations with his allegiance to his home state of Arizona, all within the extremely complex political, economic, social, and corporate welter that surrounded the apportionment of the Colorado River.

STEWART UDALL: "Well, I was on the hot seat with regard to the Colorado River Project, which was really the [Central] Arizona Project. After the Supreme Court [decision] in 1963, Arizona then was going to have a shot to get its big project. You have to historically look at the biggest water fight in the West between big California and little Arizona. Neither of these states contributed a great deal of water to the river. The main contribution from Arizona was the Gila River, which originates in the mountains in Arizona and New Mexico. Arizona, although they walked away from Santa Fe [Colorado River Compact of 1922], they didn't agree. They were given a pretty good allocation of water, but afterwards, when you got to the 1940s, California already had its [Colorado River] aqueduct on the river, and Hoover Dam had been built. Arizona wasn't getting much benefit. So Arizona wanted to have its big project, and they had the Bureau of Reclamation study various alternatives. What should be done? When they brought that to the floor of Congress in 1951 and '52, Senator Carl Hayden [from Arizona] was a very powerful figure in the Appropriations Committee. Arizona then had for two years the Senate majority leader. They passed it right through the Senate. They just whipped it through. California blocked it. That was their strategy. The longer they could keep Arizona off the river, the longer they could use water they weren't entitled to, you see. And that was what created a lot of enmity and a lot of suspicion in Arizona. And California blocked the legislation in the House. California was throwing its weight around and said, 'No. Arizona's water internally hadn't been qualified.' And there were disputes with California. They had to go to the Supreme Court. Well, that was a nice strategy because it bought eleven years of delay. That was finally resolved by the Supreme Court who confirmed Arizona's contention in 1963. Then Arizona's project could start to move forward."

The secretary of the interior is the majordomo, or water master, in the lower basin of the Colorado River. Arizona's annual allocation is 2.8 million acre-feet of water. Nevada's is a modest 300,000 acre-feet. California is entitled to 4.4 million acre-feet. Colorado River scholar Norris Hundley addressed some of the fine points that shaped the apportionment of the Colorado River.

Norris Hundley: "An important thing to remember in connection with this 4.4 [million acre-feet] minimum is that California can't be deprived of that 4.4 million. They could be deprived if the river drops down to the point where there is not anything more than 4 million acre-feet in the basin. Then it is only going to get four. But Nevada has to get its share. As a practical matter, California can't be deprived of the 4.4 million acre-feet, and what makes that practically possible is that Arizona has bound itself never to deprive California of that 4.4, even if it can't get its 2.8 million. It has obligated itself to make sure that California gets 4.4 even if it means Arizona can not get 2.8. Why? That is the price Arizona paid to get the Central Arizona Project, which was approved in 1968. California controlled enough votes that Arizona would never get the Central Arizona Project approved unless Arizona cut a deal. And the deal was that Arizona had to obligate itself to serve as insurance for California's 4.4."

Charles Wilkinson is an attorney on the faculty of the University of Colorado in Boulder. He revealed his passionate interest in the history of the intense conflict between California and Arizona over Colorado River water.

Charles Wilkinson: "The competition really started in the nineteenth century. When Arizona became a state in 1912, it knew that it had a fast-growing competitor to the West in the form of California. And it also feared the other five states in the watershed. Early on, Arizona decided, not wanting any limits, to just use every last drop of its Colorado River water. And they were afraid, and they had reasonable fears because of the system, that if they didn't use it, someone else would. And so, you have a really good mixture of paranoia, avarice, waste, technology, because a lot of the development was done with very high levels of technology, and certainly lack of concern for the river as a river. Arizona and California fighting over the Colorado River were in the Supreme Court of the United States five times. And finally, Arizona got its water right established to the Colorado River in that famous 1963 decision. Arizona wanted to put that water to use as quickly as it could. It was very well positioned. It had Carl Hayden in the Senate, the most senior member of the Senate. He had been serving since statehood. It had the secretary of the interior [Stewart Udall], who under law has very broad authority over Colorado River water."

STEWART UDALL: "After the war, after World War II, California had its big project, Hoover Dam. The upper-basin states, as they were called, decided they wanted to begin dams, irrigation projects, hydroelectric dams, primarily, to provide benefits and uses of water. They would tell the Bureau of Reclamation, 'Go study where hydro-dams should be built. Go study and tell us how to control the river so we can keep some of the water in our states.' I am talking about the upper-basin states. And the Bureau of Reclamation would do this, and they put together what was called the upper Colorado River Storage Project. It had a dam in Echo Park that would encroach on a national monument and that immediately started a controversy. That is where the Sierra Club took off and became a national organization under David Brower's leadership."

David Brower had a lot of help from Martin Litton, an early environmentalist and white-water river runner who loves the wild country and the wild rivers of the West. He was also a journalist and photographer who worked for the *Los Angeles Times*. I visited with this great adventurer at his home in California, where he told me about how he and Brower came to join forces in the mid-twentieth century to thwart construction of the Split Mountain and Echo Park dams on the upper Green River, which would have flooded parts of Dinosaur National Monument in Utah and Wyoming.

MARTIN LITTON: "I got a call from David Brower, whom I didn't know, but I think I had heard of him. It was 1952. That is when he became executive director of the Sierra Club. And he had heard of me because he had seen these articles in the *Los Angeles Times* I had been running, which were pretty rabid. They were pro—natural environment, and nothing else. He wanted me to come and join him in doing great things with the Sierra Club. He was on fire. And we decided to get together and work together on this within the Sierra Club in stopping the Split Mountain and Echo Park dams in Dinosaur National Monument. The Sierra Club achieved its first real conservation victory in those four years. We sit back, and I am very much a part of it by then, and say, 'My God, how did that happen? We saved Dinosaur.' In saving Dinosaur, you are not just talking about a quarry with dinosaur bones in it. You are talking about a vast magnificent area that is as worthy of any kind of attention as any other national park. There is a symbolism to it."

When Floyd Dominy was commissioner of the Bureau of Reclamation in the mid-twentieth century, he was relentless in his pursuit of greening up the landscape of the arid West by building dams to provide water for countless irrigation projects and to generate hydroelectricity for both pumping water and providing electricity to the cities of the West.

FLOYD DOMINY: "A lot of people get confused. They think that Echo Park was a substitute for Glen Canyon or that Glen Canyon was a substitute for Echo Park. Actually Glen Canyon Dam would have been needed whether or not Echo Park and Split Mountain were authorized. They were strictly 'cash register' dams that were on the Green River. They didn't provide the huge carryover storage that was required that Glen Canyon would do. Now it is said that it is just a matter of poor nomenclature that they got defeated. If they would have been called to Rattlesnake Butte, Snake Hollow, we could have got them authorized. But to talk about Echo Park and Split Mountain it was a bad nomenclature. At any rate, Dave Brower and company had beat the bureau hands down on that one."

MARTIN LITTON: "You win something, you tend to sit back on your hands, relax, and congratulate yourself. But meanwhile, the whole Colorado River system was being threatened by all kinds of desecration—diversions, mostly by dams, manipulation of those streams, the Colorado main stem. And of course, what the main stem is made of is all the tributaries that come in. And those are being worked to death for human gain, for profit on the part of somebody. Every politician had his finger in the pie, trying to satisfy his constituents' needs. His constituents put him in office, they paved the trail, so to speak. And he is going to respond to them, even though many of them were corporate constituents, and those kinds tend to destroy our Earth rather than help it."

CHARLES WILKINSON: "As the '60s developed, after Arizona got its water right, it was going to have the Central Arizona Project which was going to bring water from the Colorado over to Phoenix and Tucson by means of a pipeline. Arizona was pushing hard for that. Well, Wayne Aspinall was chair of the House Interior Committee at that time. Wayne Aspinall held a lock on all legislation, and he wasn't going to let the bill go through unless Colorado got its water projects. Aspinall laid up five of them, and this piece of legislation was going to go through. In fact, every one of the states in the watershed had projects they wanted, and it was a very delicate balance. But right at the heart of it was the Central Arizona Project.

"Water projects always have engineering obstacles. Things like drilling under the Continental Divide, or transporting water 200 miles from Mono Lake down to Los Angeles. These are big projects. Well, the Central Arizona Project had the obstacle of distance. But it also had the obstacle of gradient. And a good part of that line, from the Colorado River over to Phoenix and then to Tucson, was up-hill. In addition to pumping water a long distance, you had to pump it uphill. That wasn't going to stop anybody. When you have got a big-time western development project in that era, nothing is going to stop it. The obstacle of gradient wasn't going to stop it. And in fact, the answer was simple. Dam the Grand Canyon. Plug the Grand Canyon. Perfect for a reservoir. Build up a big head of water behind a couple of dams, and you have got hydropower to fuel the uphill climb of the Central Arizona Project. Oh, it was so simple."

FLOYD DOMINY: "The bureau [of Reclamation] had been studying these means of supplying that water out of the Colorado River into central Arizona. Then we had determined that the water could be pumped out of Lake Havasu and carried across the country in lined canals, reaching Phoenix and Tucson. Of course we recognize that this is a very expensive project. And we had visualized that we got the hydroelectric dams below Glen Canyon Dam, one above the [Grand Canyon] national park, and one below the Grand Canyon National Park, to be the 'cash register' dams to underwrite the huge cost for this project."

CHARLES WILKINSON: "By the 1960s, however, simplicity wasn't as simple as it might have been a generation ago. The fly in the ointment, the ultimate pain in the ass, was David Brower. And Brower had this crazy idea that we shouldn't just dam the Grand Canyon, that it was a living canyon, and a living river. It was immoral and bad economics, and bad common sense, and bad humanity to do that. And bad beauty. And Brower got up on his hind legs in the way that only he could, and he stopped the damming of the Grand Canyon."

David Brower and I became friends in 1970 when we were working jointly on environmental issues that gravely affected the American Southwest. We remained friends throughout the rest of his lifetime. I regard him as one of America's greatest heroes. I recorded a conversation with David at his home in

Berkeley, California, where he related that after he and the Sierra Club defeated the proposed Echo Park and Split Mountain dams on the upper Green River, he was forced to address the so-called "cash register" dams intended to be built at Bridge Canyon and Marble Canyon on either end of the Grand Canyon.

DAVID BROWER: "I became aware of the Grand Canyon dams when I got interested in the Colorado River, prior to the struggle over Dinosaur National Monument. We knew that the Bureau of Reclamation wanted to build some dams. And once the Arizona–California suit had been settled by the Supreme Court, there would be some further development. We didn't know quite what it would be. But we did have proposals for the Grand Canyon dams, both of them, and in 1949, when I was on the Sierra Club board of directors, I voted for both dams. We found out later that it was a mistake to vote for those dams, and that we had been led down the primrose trail, that there would be enormous damage to the river itself, and the life zones along the river, as well as the most beautiful part of the scenery, the living river. And the next year, we withdrew our support of that dam. Ever since then I have been opposed to those dams, and any other dams in the Colorado River with my big slip, when I was at least momentarily for not only Glen Canyon Dam but a taller Glen Canyon Dam. That is a story I would rather forget."

FLOYD DOMINY: "This is the time when Admiral Rickover and Glen Seymour were making wild claims about atomic power, and how cheap it was going to be. Seymour was telling committees at Congress that atomic power was going to be so cheap that you wouldn't have to meter it. Going to be so cheap you could desalt seawater and irrigate with it. So Congress was telling me, 'Well, why do we need any more hydroelectric dams, Commissioner? You are passé. We are in the atomic age now.' They were the ones that defeated the Bridge Canyon Dam. And I had come to the conclusion that we could give up on Marble. Marble was the lesser of the two as far as production of power. The rest is history, of course. We didn't get the authorization as proposed.

"The compromise to building Bridge Canyon Dam was to build a huge coal-fired plant, partly underwritten by the federal government and the rest of it by the Salt River Project and other power users. Power developers. The pumping power to pump the water for the Central Arizona Project comes from this coal-fired plant. You can visualize a plant that burns a trainload of coal a day—that is how big it is: 2.5 million kilowatt capacity. The government is invested in that proposal in order to have power for the Central Arizona Project."

DAVID BROWER: "I kept learning. I first thought that you could save a lot of rivers by going to nuclear power. Then I found that was no good. So I was willing to save rivers by going to coal, and found that was no good. And I finally smartened up and found out the way to save rivers and coal, and avoid nuclear power, is to take a whole new look at our ideas about economic growth, and to ask the essential questions: 'What kind of economic growth must we have? And what kind can we, and the Earth, no longer afford?' And that is where my thinking has been ever since the Colorado project."

Bruce Babbitt was secretary of the interior throughout the 1990s during the Clinton administration. As water master of the lower Colorado River, he inherited the legacy of controversy that continues to abound over allocation of water.

BRUCE BABBITT: "I start thinking of Lake Powell by remembering David Brower. He was a great environmentalist, a great American, and he died with a very guilty conscience about Glen Canyon. That dates back really to the fight over the dam at Dinosaur [National Monument]. The compromise was, 'We will move it downstream to Glen Canyon.' And it was only later that David and others realized that it was a bigger sacrifice than the original site at Dinosaur, and that in fact it really wasn't necessary to build a dam at either place. The logic for Glen Canyon Dam was embodied not on the land but in a legal document in the Colorado River Compact. It was driven by this kind of Talmudic discussion about shares and delivery requirements."

The 1922 Colorado River Compact actually set the stage for construction of the Glen Canyon Dam. When I interviewed Rick Gold in 2001, he was the deputy director of the Upper Colorado Region. He reiterated how the Law of the River inevitably led to the presence of the Glen Canyon Dam and Lake Powell.

RICK GOLD: "What happens at Glen Canyon Dam is that it is there. It has about 25 million acre-feet of water in storage, and it allows the upper-basin states of Colorado, Utah, Wyoming, and New Mexico to utilize their Colorado River water supplies, as allocated to them by the 1922 [Colorado River] Compact, and among them in the 1948 Upper [Colorado River] Basin Compact. Without that storage, if that storage were not there, after a year of two of consecutive drought, like we are in today, you could see the lower basin with its priority call seeking the release of upper-basin water. And if it were not in storage to release, the only choice is to curtail upper-basin development. So most of the cities in the upper basin—cities and farms, agriculture and industry that enjoy the benefits of just diverting water from the Colorado River or its tributaries—would have to be cut back in order for the upper-basin states to meet the downstream call at Lee's Ferry. The compact is pretty specific in that it requires 75 million acre-feet in any ten-year period, or an average of about 7.5 million acre-feet plus the shortfall in making up the Mexican depletion.

"So the target release of 8.23 million acre-feet at Lee's Ferry would be very difficult to meet without a storage reservoir. So assuming that someone were seriously considering draining Lake Powell, the impact is that you would be calling out states like Colorado and New Mexico from diverting their apportioned water supplies of the Colorado River because there would be no storage for the upper basin to meet its downstream requirement."

CHARLES WILKINSON: "Incredibly enough, even with the wild subsidies of the Hardrock Mining [and Reclamation] Act, you still have to pay a minimal fee to get a patent to a mining claim. But water is free. And you may have to transport it. And you may have to build a large canal from the Colorado River over to Los Angeles or a pipeline from the Colorado River over to Phoenix and Tucson. But the water itself is free. We have this high-sounding language about water. But we have never lived up to it. And what we have really done is just opened the rivers for a very competitive race between individuals and between states. First in time, first in right. And you can take all you want. You can dry rivers up. Of course the main river itself, in most years, when it hits the Gulf of California [Sea of Cortés] is dry. And so we have given no heed to the rivers as rivers. And we have given no heed to the value of water. In fact, we've given it away on the cheap."

By the 1970s the environmental movement had gained a foothold in American culture. It was during this time that both the National Environmental Policy Act and the Endangered Species Act were signed. These acts confronted our society with the effect of continuous development without considering probable consequences. They forced us to examine the effects of resource extraction and development on the natural environment, and the possible jeopardy to other species with which we share our habitat. In 2001, attorney Pam Hyde was the executive director of policy for Southwest Rivers, and is part of a growing movement to decommission the Glen Canyon Dam and drain Lake Powell. She describes the horns of the dilemma.

PAM HYDE: "The difficulty now is that we are going back and saying that the way that the law is set up continues to allow for consumptive uses, diversions out of the river, without any real recognition of what the environmental consequences of those actions are. And the only things that we have to work with now to try and reset that balance are the Endangered Species Act and the National Environmental Policy Act. It is a real question mark still as to which laws prevail. I mean, if you are putting the Endangered Species Act up against, say, the Colorado River Storage Project Act, does water development prevail? Or does the endangered species protection prevail? And it is still just not clear. One of the fears of the environmental community is if you actually ask that question, you might not get the answer that you want. And then you have nothing left to try and push for environmental protection."

Thus we have reached the heart of the conflict. As a culture, we have pursued an economic paradigm of "growth for the sake of growth" within a planetary habitat of finite resources. If we continue to grow, we shall run out of resources and possibly go extinct, an irreversible condition. However, if we stay the juggernaut, we have a chance to wend our way back to balance. We have a system of laws within which we culturally comport ourselves. Some of these laws are at absolute loggerheads, to wit: the Colorado River Compact of 1922 and the National Environmental Policy Act.

My old *compañero* Edward Abbey coined the apothegm: "Growth for the sake of growth is the ideology of the cancer cell." Are we indeed metastasizing across the face of the planet? Are we so far removed from the wisdom required of our species to persist equitably with our habitat that we fail to recognize the folly born of erroneous legislation?

We'll soon know because the evidence that prevails indicates that we have initiated a spasm of extinction of species of the magnitude that carried away the dinosaurs 65 million years or so ago.

Cultural diversity and biodiversity are inextricably interlinked. Cognitive diversity is to be nurtured and gleaned. Science and technology alone will not save us. We must tap into another wellspring to revitalize our ailing culture. We must look to cultures that evolved as their habitats evolved and try to understand their perspective—and then meld that wisdom with our scientific and technological applications, and be relentless in our self-discipline. Otherwise, *Adios y buena suerte*.

v.

By the middle of the twentieth century, America had suffered through two world wars and the Great Depression. In 1929, our cultural psyche plummeted with the stock market crash that dominated the next eleven years. Former secretary of commerce Herbert Hoover, who had presided over the historic 1922 Colorado River Compact meeting in Santa Fe, had been elected to the presidency in 1928 as a Republican. He was defeated in 1932 by New York governor Franklin Delano Roosevelt, a forward-thinking Democrat who initiated the New Deal in a massive attempt at economic recovery. The New Deal resulted in creating enormous public works projects that included the Tennessee Valley Authority, the Civilian Conservation Corps, the Works Progress Administration, and myriad other means of employing the American out-of-work labor force.

Rural residents of the American West, while indeed affected by the Great Depression, were not as hard hit as urban dwellers whose jobs evaporated as businesses that employed them withered and folded. Many rural residents were able to subsist because they could still farm or pursue cattle and sheep ranching. The Hopi and Navajo Indians of the Southwest were probably the least affected because they were still so aligned with their traditional subsistence ways of life, and the collapse of American economics struck them a stout but glancing blow.

Newcomers to the West were hot on the trail of greening up the arid landscape west of the hundredth meridian. Thus western politicians were intent on serving their rural constituencies by invoking major acts of Congress to put every square inch of landscape to "best use."

Earlier in the century, the Reclamation Act of 1902 resulted in great irrigation projects throughout the arid West. Stewart Udall shared his thoughts regarding the success of Arizona's Salt River Project, which later served as a model for combining water and electricity in dam construction in the West and for the Central Arizona Project.

STEWART UDALL: "The Salt River Project was not only one of the pioneering western irrigation projects but one of the most successful. That dam [Theodore Roosevelt Dam] was completed in 1913. The Salt River Project is an irrigation project. That huge farming area near Mesa, Arizona, and the surrounding area—the farms fed off the canals that came out of the Roosevelt Dam, and even on into Phoenix itself, and Glendale. Those huge canals were taking this water. These were very productive farms. And that was one of the most successful irrigation projects. They also developed hydroelectric power. The Salt River Project transformed the Phoenix area. When they first developed the Central Arizona Project, the model was the Salt River Project of 1913. We told Congress, and I testified many times as secretary of the interior, that this was going to be based on the success of the Salt River Project. And the water being brought in would be used for farming."

In order to accomplish the Central Arizona Project, an enormous amount of energy would be required to pump water uphill, all the way from Lake Havasu on the Colorado River to the central valleys of Arizona. Bruce Babbitt reiterated a bit of the history of the quest for electricity to power the pumps.

BRUCE BABBITT: "The original idea was that the dams at Marble and Bridge canyons, at the upper and lower ends of the Grand Canyon, were going to provide the 'cash register' to pull the water up in central Arizona. That fight was won [to stop the dams from being constructed], and David Brower really vindicated himself here, because that fight resulted in the cancellation of two dams, and no substitutes. But there was a substitute. There was a coal-burning power plant on the Colorado Plateau at the Navajo Generating Station at Page."

Attorney William Swan, who has practiced river law and knows the human history of the Colorado River, revealed that the time was perfect for the Central Arizona Project to receive congressional support.

WILLIAM SWAN: "Congress was still in the mood for projects. And that was still the thinking of our society that that was the right thing to do, to build these things. And of course, there was already a lake there, as we have discussed, in the form of Parker Dam in Lake Havasu, because that is where the Metropolitan Water District was pumping out to the west. And so, Arizona simply put its big pumping system there into that lake on the eastern shore, and then started building the big massive canals and pumping plants to central Arizona."

In post–World War II America, Sunbelt cities—including Phoenix, San Diego, and Los Angeles—were like magnets. House-building boomed, and many politicians and developers had their eyes on the Colorado Plateau as a major source of water and energy. Attorney Charles Wilkinson shared his very clear insight into what he calls the "big buildup."

CHARLES WILKINSON: "An omnibus bill began to develop. This was during the 'big buildup' of the Colorado Plateau, the interior part of the watershed. The canyon country, the red rock country, the Four Corners area, and the cities that surrounded the Colorado Plateau in an arc from Salt Lake City to Denver over to Santa Fe and Albuquerque down to El Paso, Phoenix, and Tucson, Las Vegas, to Southern California cities, they all needed to develop like Phoenix. They all had used up their own water supplies, and they weren't going to build coal plants near the cities because coal-fired plants were too dirty. And so [they looked to] the Colorado Plateau, the interior country, which was dry country, but still had the biggest river in the Southwest running down through it, and deep canyons, which made for great reservoirs to store water, and big coal deposits, and big uranium deposits. The raid was on. About a third of it was Indian country. Most of the rest of it was public lands, and as far as the cities were concerned, that ended their competition [between themselves]. It is not fully appreciated, but that was a key point. They ended their competition, joined together, used [the Department of the] Interior as one-stop shopping, because Interior had control over both the public lands and the Indian lands, and effectively the river itself. And the big buildup was one of the, if not the largest peacetime industrial buildups in the history of the world. Between about 1955 and 1975."

WILLIAM deBuys: "I think Charles Wilkinson conceptualized things exactly right, that Glen Canyon Dam is the lynchpin of the 'big buildup.' the big postwar buildup. And its power production made possible the metastasis of Phoenix. Its water led in all kinds of different ways to all kinds of different things. And if it weren't for Glen Canyon Dam, the Sunbelt phenomenon would not have taken place. Not the way it did."

STEWART UDALL: "What Phoenix has ended up doing, like Southern California did, the land was more valuable for developing subdivisions. And with this enormous growth of Phoenix trying to be another Los Angeles, the farmers sold out, and they tore down the citrus groves and cotton fields. And you see now this huge glob of urban sprawl. By the time the project was finished, it was so costly the farmers couldn't afford the water. And the water's primary use now is for urban use. And it may end up rescuing Tucson, which has grown too far and too fast. The idea of this huge water project, pumping the water in over the hills from the Colorado River, was in itself a huge venture. And we sold it to Congress and the country as a way to preserve this very productive agricultural land. Now the water is there and the aqueducts are available. It is costly water. It is much more costly than anybody imagined. And we certainly misled Congress, in my opinion, on this. So the cities are going to get that water, ultimately, and they will have to pay for the project."

The cost of the Central Arizona Project came in at around $5 billion. Many years ago, David Brower told me that early on, he had major misgivings about the Central Arizona Project.

DAVID BROWER: "I think we foresaw that, way back in the early 1950s that this was just a ploy to get water essentially for agricultural use, but to switch it to domestic use and to industrial use as soon as they could get their hands on it. They were getting it with an enormous subsidy, and back in these old days, I did a lot of calculating. By the time you put the interest costs in, the normal interest cost that the government was paying for their money and was not collecting from the farmers, you found a huge subsidy per acre to get the water on it. I know it is frightfully expensive, and we could count on the developers getting hold of the water one way or the other. I didn't know the speed with which they were going to do it in the Sunbelt, in Arizona and everywhere else, where people started to move because they like to stay warm."

For many years, Charles Wilkinson worked with the Native American Rights Fund, whose legal staff worked closely with Hopi and Navajo Indians to thwart the Peabody Coal Company of East St. Louis from strip-mining coal on land sacred to both tribes. His passion on behalf of his Hopi and Navajo friends is enduring.

CHARLES WILKINSON: "You've gotta have the CAP [Central Arizona Project]. And that was not only nonnegotiable but non-discussible. That means you had to have another power source. Now the simple solution [to damming the Grand Canyon] was the great, world-class coal deposit under Black Mesa [in northern Arizona]. Black Mesa had obstacles that should have been as obvious and as important as the distance and the gradient of the CAP itself. But they weren't. What the obstacles should have been but weren't is that this is the Hopis' ancestral land. The Hopis are a deeply traditional tribe in one of the most remote areas in the Lower 48, living in their own way and deeply connected to Black Mesa. It is a very complicated matter to scour out the coal bed and create one of the largest, if not the largest, coal-mining facility in the world, and then send the coal to two different power plants. One, the Mojave over in Nevada, would be used for electricity, generally. The coal would also be shipped north, to Page [Arizona], where the Navajo Generating Station would be built to provide the electricity for the CAP, which was far to the south. But with the power grid that had been built up during the big buildup, that was of no consequence. That 'simple' formula—use Black Mesa coal, ship it north to the Navajo Generating Station, use that electricity for the CAP—should have been profoundly complicated for us. Because you are tearing up Hopi land. You are tearing up old villages, sacred sites. You are then sending it to a coal-fired power plant that was going to foul the skies, the Hopi skies, and everyone else's skies. It got even more tangled, and even more dark, because of the way that the Hopi lease with Peabody Coal was negotiated."

Before the onset of the Great Depression, the U.S. government policy regarding Indians was to turn them into white folks by educating them to the white man's ways in Bureau of Indian Affairs (BIA) boarding schools. While attending these boarding schools, the Indians were forbidden to speak in their native tongues, and they were taught that their traditional lifeways were worse than valueless. Every attempt was made to drill their religions and cultural traditions out of their minds and souls. They rarely were allowed to go to their homes and their parents. If they were overheard uttering even a few syllables that smacked of tribal lingo, they were beaten. There were yet U.S. military veterans of the Indian Wars of the late nineteenth century abroad, and it was still not uncommon to hear the familiar apothegm of yore: "The only good Indian is a dead Indian."

With Roosevelt's New Deal, the BIA was mandated to treat Indians with respect for themselves as individuals and as members of tribal groups in order that their cultures not disappear from the face of the land. John Collier was appointed as commissioner of the Bureau of Indian Affairs, and he appointed Oliver La Farge, author of the classic novel *Laughing Boy*, to represent the BIA in Hopi country. La Farge's main job was to get the Hopis to vote for a tribal constitution to result in the creation of a tribal government after the model of that of the U.S. government. After considerable cajoling and seemingly endless attempts to persuade the Hopis to participate in this process, La Farge succeeded in setting up a tribal vote. Even though only 15 percent of the Hopis voted, an insufficient number according to BIA criteria, it was enough to result in the establishment of the Hopi Tribal Council.

The Hopis traditionally live in autonomous villages on promontories extending southward from Black Mesa. They select leaders from among themselves known as *kikmongwis*. Traditionally they do not vote but are self-governed through consensus. They have followed their cultural traditions for at least a thousand years. The notion of voting was abhorrent to traditional Hopis. By not voting in the election they were expressing their disapproval for adopting a constitution and tribal council.

However, in October 1936 the election was held with 651 of the estimated 4,500 Hopis voting, the BIA claimed that it was satisfied, and the constitution was approved by Secretary of the Interior Harold Ickes in December 1936.

In a document entitled "Report to the Kikmongwis" prepared by the Indian Law Resource Center in Washington, D.C., in 1979, Oliver La Farge is cited as writing in his notes:

> It is alien to the Hopis to settle matters out of hand by majority vote. Such a vote leaves a dissatisfied minority which makes them very uneasy. Their natural way of doing is to discuss among themselves at great length and group by group until public opinion as a whole has settled overwhelmingly in one direction. It is during this process, too, that the Kikmongwis can exert influence without entering into disputes. In actual practice this system is democratic, but it works differently from ours. Opposition is expressed by abstention. Those who are against something stay away from meetings at which it is to be discussed and generally refuse to vote on it.

The original tribal council lasted only seven years before the overriding will of the Hopi people caused it to disintegrate. However, as mineral companies gained increasing interest in what lay beneath the surface of the Hopis' sacred landscape, the government was compelled to resurrect the tribal council, to the exclusion of the tribal religious leaders, so that the Hopi tribe would have a legally recognized entity with which to negotiate mineral extraction contracts.

And so it was that the BIA was able to restore the Hopi Tribal Council in late 1950, and thus establish a bureaucratic system whereby Hopi signatures might legally sign away Hopi mineral rights for modest monetary return—hence transforming sacred habitat into money. In 1951, attorney John Boyden was appointed as claims attorney for the Hopi tribe, thus insinuating himself in the catbird seat between the chancellors of the exchequers of the mining industry and the Hopi

Tribal Council. As the years wore on and the Central Arizona Project gained momentum, revealing the need for cheap coal to fire the Navajo Generating Station to supply electricity to pump water from Lake Havasu to the central valleys of Arizona, this sinister Salt Lake City lawyer hovered like a hungry raven ever ready to snatch morsels of lucre as it passed from one hand to another as he conducted negotiations between mining conglomerates, including the Peabody Coal Company, and the Hopi Tribal Council—the not quite legitimate front for the Hopi tribe.

In a recorded conversation in 1984, I asked my old friend Stewart Udall, a man of great integrity who has devoted his life to the highest good, if he could cast light on the Boyden debacle.

STEWART UDALL: "Well, I learned of this long afterward. In fact, I learned it for the first time just a few years ago, and I was rather taken aback. I always thought Boyden, because he was the Mormon elder kind of person, was within his own lights an honest man. And this would have said that he was engaged in some questionable and devious activities, and that maybe his main interest was representing other clients—that he had a conflict of interest because he had to run the approval that was obtained for the Black Mesa coal development through the tribal government that existed at that time. But if he was simultaneously being paid by the Peabody Coal Company, this is what we would call a very blatant conflict of interest in white man's society, by any standard."

Vernon Masayesva was a young man when giant earthmovers began to strip-mine Black Mesa. He revealed to me his perspective regarding the dark side of the so-called contract between the Peabody Coal Company and the Hopi Tribal Council.

VERNON MASAYESVA: "Our attorney John Boyden played this little game of pretending to have us involved. But as we learned later on, everything was already pretty much set. Our attorney was working with the government, with the power companies. And they were going to mine the coal. So, Mr. Boyden, who is now dead, up front said, 'I am here in behalf of Peabody Coal Company.' He had just negotiated a lease with Peabody, and he was our general counsel."

CHARLES WILKINSON: "The Hopi's lawyer in the mid-'60s, who had been their lawyer since the late '40s and would die in '81, was John Boyden, a leading Salt Lake City lawyer, widely respected at the time and twice candidate for governor [of Utah]. The lease with Peabody that the Hopis signed in 1966 was a terrible financial transaction for the Hopis. The lease of coal was far below market value. The lease of water was below $2 an acre-foot at a time when it was worth $300 an acre-foot, or more. And there were many, many prerogatives that Peabody received in leasing that coal and extensions of greater lease areas, and greater lengths of time to do the mining, that Peabody obtained for little or no compensation to the Hopis. It was a terrible transaction. The Hopis, if they were going to lease their traditional land, should not have received just a lease of market value. Instead, it should have been way above market value because the Hopis had such leverage, because the 'Christmas Tree' legislation that was going through, that was going to benefit the industries of seven different states, depended on Black Mesa coal. Because the bill couldn't go through without the CAP [Central Arizona Project] and the CAP couldn't go through without this source of electricity to pump the water uphill. And so the Hopis had great leverage, and John Boyden well knew about the big buildup, and well knew about the way that the Southwest was booming, and the way it had focused in on the Colorado Plateau, and the way in which the Hopis had so much leverage. But instead of having a highly favorable business deal or even a business deal at 'market value,' the Hopis had a dreadful business deal. And there had always been rumors that John Boyden had secretly, in the dark, represented Peabody Coal."

These rumors were verified, and documentation of John Boyden's conflict of interest appears in Charles Wilkinson's excellent book *Fire on the Plateau*.

By early 1970, my esteemed pal William E. Brown, then the National Park Service historian for the Southwest, came to me with the news that indeed a giant coal strip mine was imminently scheduled for Black Mesa, sacred homeland to the Hopis and known as the body of the Female Mountain to the Navajos. Bill and I immediately drove out to Black Mesa from Santa Fe, drove its length over rutted dirt roads, and then rented a plane and flew over this landscape. We camped at a remote site overlooking the North Rim of the Grand Canyon, and it was there that Bill wrote "The Rape of Black Mesa," the first article to be published about the forthcoming debacle.

On returning home to Santa Fe, we formed the Black Mesa Defense Fund. We were but a small coterie of self-appointed radical environmentalists that included Jimmy Hopper, Terry Moore, Phil Shultz, Harvey Mudd, Caroline Rackley, Tom Andrews, Abigail Adler, Hannah Hibbs, Peggy Swift, and, peripherally, Dave Foreman, Alvin Josephy, and Edward Abbey. In April, I went to visit my old friend David Monongye, one the key religious leaders of the Hopi tribe. I told him about what was intended for Black Mesa. He immediately called for an assemblage of traditional Hopi elders that met in Shungopovi on Second Mesa. He asked me to speak about the intended mine.

I stood before sixty-three tribal elders and told them that my heretofore meager research had revealed that an enormous coal strip mine was intended to begin operation on Black Mesa, and that the coal would be shipped via an as-yet-to-be constructed railroad across the Kaibito Plateau to the Navajo Generating Station that would soon be constructed near the shores of Lake Powell, the enormous storage reservoir behind the Glen Canyon Dam. Coal would also be slurried in a pipeline using pristine water pumped from the aquifer beneath Black Mesa to the already existing Mojave Generating Station in Laughlin, Nevada. I told them that the arrangements already negotiated by tribal attorney John Boyden with the Peabody Coal Company had been approved by their tribal council.

The Hopi elders rose as a single, infuriated body, their faces contorted with anger and pain. Gradually they quieted down. The only other Anglos present (or *bahannas* as the Hopis call white folks) were a hydrologist and Peggy Swift, a freelance journalist. The hydrologist went on to describe how the pumping of water from the aquifer at the rate of 2,000 gallons per minute could seriously affect the Hopi springs, their only source of water other than the sparse rains that sprinkled but ten inches of precipitation a year.

During that meeting, I was introduced to Thomas Banyacya, appointed by the traditionalists as interpreter because his English was very good. I also met John and Mina Lansa. Mina was the kikmongwi for Oraibi, which is believed to be the oldest continuously inhabited village on the North American continent. I met several other Hopi elders all of whom would become friends, some even close friends, over the next few years. They asked if the Black Mesa Defense Fund would help them stop what was happening on Black Mesa. I said we would try. We tried every legal means. We failed over the long haul, which I deeply rue to this day.

The traditional Hopis took their plight to attorneys—including Joe Brescher, Bruce Green, John Echohawk, and others at the Native American Rights Fund in Boulder, Colorado—all of whom fought a battle decidedly stacked against them in a vain attempt to halt the desecration of the sacred landscape of Black Mesa. For years the legal battles waged, but congressional legislation serves those who fund it, and the Central Arizona Project would not be denied its political due.

And so the strip mine at Black Mesa continues to this day to be carved as a great ever-widening wound in the body of the Female Mountain. Vernon Masayesva and a coterie of young Hopis have fought incessantly to thwart the pumping of water to slurry coal to the Mojave Generating Station in Nevada.

VERNON MASAYESVA: "Southern Cal Edison had a small power plant up in Nevada. So he [John Boyden] must have convinced them to upgrade the plant and make it bigger. And he would give them the coal. Cheap. It is going to have to go 273 miles. That is when they came out with the idea of slurrying the water. Grinding up coal, mixing it with pristine water, half coal, half water, and pipe it over a distance of 273 miles. That is a long way to be hauling coal. And to make it cheap, the water was sold for $1.67 an acre-foot. From a very ancient aquifer, geologists call Navajo Aquifer. That is where it would come from. The lease does not specify where the water would come from. It also had no limit as to how much can be used. So this kind of left the door open for the mining company to tap into the best water. And the reason for using the best water as opposed to a highly mineralized water, they would much prefer to use pristine water. Pristine, meaning soft water. It is the best water you can find anywhere in the world. It is 35,000 years old. It was put there during the Ice Age. The company wanted to use this water so it would not corrode the pipelines as fast. Brackish water would do that. And to make it economically feasible, Hopis were forced to subsidize the operation, along with the Navajos. The subsidies came in a form of cheap rate: $1.67. There are no records anywhere where the Hopi tribe has approved the sale of water for $1.67 per acre-foot."

John Echohawk is the director of the Native American Rights Fund, and has long been involved in the Black Mesa controversy. He told me about the impact the deep wells were having on the Navajo Aquifer in the area around Black Mesa.

JOHN ECHOHAWK: "Peabody always claimed that this water came from an aquifer so deep that it wouldn't really impact the environment around there. And of course, over the thirty years or so that it has been operating, people living there have started to see that there is an impact. Their groundwater is drying up. What Vernon would like to do is to get Peabody to stop doing that, and save that aquifer, and stop the change in ecosystem that is going on there by piping water in from Lake Powell for the Peabody Coal Company to operate that slurry pipeline. The water is now pumped at the rate of 3.3 million gallons per day, which amounts to about 1.3 billion gallons annually."

At the time of writing, Peabody Coal Company has stopped pumping water out of the Black Mesa aquifer, and the Mohave Generating Station has ceased to operate. Vernon Masayesva and other Hopis devoted years of their lives to protecting their endangered aquifer so that their culture could continue to live in their traditional homeland.

Arizona is home to many Native American cultures whose water rights are just now being adjudicated.

JOHN ECHOHAWK: "The Central Arizona Project and its power needs are being taken care of, in large part, by the development of the Navajo [Generating Station] that is fueled by Black Mesa coal that you and I were working on years ago. Of course the Central Arizona Project since that time has played and is still playing a key role in the settlement of Indian water-rights claims in central Arizona. Much of the water that comes into central Arizona through that project has turned out to be too expensive for most people. So the federal government finds itself using this water as part of its contribution to these Indian water-right settlements. Tribes in central Arizona are ending up with these waters coming from the Central Arizona Project to settle out its Indian water-rights claims. So it is really strange how all that has developed over these years."

NORRIS HUNDLEY: "Indians began to assert their rights for Colorado River water. The Supreme Court decision in 1963 said Arizona can have its 2.8 million acre-feet plus all the water in its tributaries. But despite [the fact] that it says Arizona vs. California in the title, the Indians were the ones who got a significant boost in these decisions. The courts were talking specifically about five reservations in the lower basin, but there are twenty-five reservations in the lower basin. And the court made its ruling in such a way that this decision would apply to all of these reservations. The courts said, 'Hey! There is an Indian water right. And it is a right to all the water that they can use to develop their reservation in terms of agriculture.' And there is no use greater of water than agriculture with one exception—a nuclear power plant.

"Some of the Indians have talked about building a nuclear power plant from time to time. And what is the total amount of the Indian water right? Well, they are still fighting it out. There are still hearings being held in courts, and when the Indians got the legal title to the water, they got legal water, paper water. But they don't have any funds to develop a project. And sometimes, because they don't have the funds from Congress anywhere to do anything, they will lease their water. Which, of course, doesn't do anything to maintain a sense of a reservation homeland."

Far to the south of Black Mesa lies the Tohono O'odham Nation that stretches from west of Tucson, Arizona, immediately adjacent to the international boundary with Mexico to Organ Pipe Cactus National Monument. This is the Sonoran Desert, regarded by many as the planet's most luxuriant desert. It is characterized by columnar cacti, palo verde, mesquite, and ironwood trees. Wildlife is abundant. The presence of the Central Arizona Project, originally conceived to serve agriculturalists, is nurturing great housing developments that now spread across the Sonoran landscape where the natural biotic community is being eradicated to make room for the burgeoning human population.

Traditionally, the Colorado River Indian Tribes include Mojave, Chemehuevi, and since the 1940s and '50s some Hopi and Navajo Indians. Their collective reservation lies along the banks of the Colorado River. They irrigate their farmlands with river water. In 2001, I interviewed Gary Hansen, an attorney who has worked with the Colorado River Indian Tribes, and who spoke of the status of Colorado Indian reservation water adjudication at that time.

GARY HANSEN: "Basically I am responsible for the management of tribes' water resources, and also their irrigation system. The Colorado River Indian Tribes have a large present perfected right in the Colorado River. They are allocated 717,148 acre-feet. They have the perfected right, which was given to them through the adjudication of the water rights by the U.S. Supreme Court. Their rights were developed and perfected because of the Winters Doctrine, which gave them the ability to get water for the amount of irrigable acres that are on their reservation. And they have about 110,000 acres of land that could be irrigated. And they irrigate about 80,000 of that. There is a major effort regarding traditional values because the tribes put a great value on the river and the natural environment that has established itself along the river. And this project here is an effort to turn back the clock and establish more of a natural environment, back the way it used to be. They have a very close tie to the habitat that has developed along the river."

In 1922, when the Colorado River Compact was enacted, Nevada had only a meager human population. Thus, it was awarded a modest allocation of only 300,000 acre-feet of Colorado River water. Today, the area around Las Vegas is the fastest-growing urban center in America. Its waters come from Lake Mead. And much of the electricity that traditionally powered the lighting arrangements of the casinos came from the nearby Mojave Generating Station that burned coal slurried through a 273-mile-long pipeline from Black Mesa. Patricia Mulroy, the general manager of the Southern Nevada Water Authority, is a clear-thinking realist, and one of the most enlightened of the so-called Colorado River "water buffaloes."

PATRICIA MULROY: "When you look at it in a macroeconomic sense, we take in 8 percent of the water resources in southern Nevada, and invest it in the industry that gives us a 75 percent gross return, 75 percent of the gross proceeds for the state of Nevada. That is not a bad investment. You need a portion of your water to sustain human life, you need a portion of your water for economic uses, and you need a portion of your water for environmental uses. Well, if you can take a mere 8 percent of your overall water supply and get a 75 percent return on that investment, that is not a bad investment. And the hotel industry has been extremely responsive. I mean, with all those water features that you see, they have done one of two things. The board, ten years ago enacted some real stringent rules about water features. Go to the basement of the Treasure Island. You will find a full-fledged wastewater treatment plant. It captures all the water. It treats it. That is what you see in those water features. Those that haven't done that, in order to build the water feature, they had to go out and they had to pay for one and a half times the amount of water they are going to use through conservation elsewhere. It works. They pay some very large water bills. Most of the water is used in the aggregate by residential users. I, as an individual user, have a hard time seeing myself as part of that larger whole, but that is who uses the water. It is people. There is a lot of talk, always, about Las Vegas as this fast-growing, out-of-control town. If you look at it historically, we are just the latest one. It is just moving up the river basin. The migration to the west has not stopped. It is just that right now, Las Vegas is the place where everybody comes. I think through the creation of the Southern Nevada Water Authority, we have set a foundation that will provide sane and sensible solutions. Managing the water resources. The community has really come together. They appreciate the need to conserve. Creating a sense of conservation by changing the ethic of an urban area as opposed to responding to a drought is a challenge. We will get there. We will get to where we need to be."

I remember flying from Las Vegas to Albuquerque one night. After the plane was aloft, it circled Las Vegas, and in the darkness, the lighting displays below were astonishing to behold. Electricity in motion, alluring to some—but not to me. As Las Vegas dropped behind, the landscape revealed little evidence of human provenance. I saw occasional headlights and only a few communities that blossomed in the night garden.

I knew when I was passing south of Black Mesa. I thought, as ever, about my Hopi friends whose land and water were being spent so that the American Southwest could be irrigated and lit. In spite of five centuries of European encroachment, the Hopis still maintain their ancient traditions of revering the Earth Mother and teaching their young about living in balance with Nature. Las Vegas and Oraibi exist as absolute extremes of human community and conduct. Hedonists and Edenists. Where lies the balance between these extremes—or can there be balance?

I know that as I have recorded the lore of the land over the decades, the utterances of my Indian friends ring true to me and reawaken my intuitions to the flow of Nature. Of course, it is ironic that many Indian reservations are now home to recently constructed casinos that lure away lucre that would otherwise be spent in Las Vegas. Revenge of the red man—or the end of wisdom?

vi.

The landscape of the American Southwest is regarded by many as one of the most beautiful on our planet. Much of it is the red rock country of the Colorado Plateau, and much of it is pure desert. One of the first things people do when they move into an area is to name the landforms. In this way, we learn the land and provide ourselves with a sense of place. In the parlances of different Indian tribes, we hear of Toroweap, Agathlan, Tsilthnaodithle, Babat Duag. The Spaniards named landmarks La Cabeza Prieta, Cerro Negro, Mesa Verde, el Río Colorado, el Río San Juan, el Río Escalante. Anglos had their day with Bears Ears, Fish Tank Canyon, Molly's Nipple, Muley Point, Comb Ridge, Lavender Canyon, Wolf Hole, and countless other names.

I have thought about the mosaic of human perspectives that this landscape has yielded and continues to yield by explorers, exploiters, and artists alike. Jim Bridger and other mountain men financed their personal adventures as they gathered pelts and hides from animals that once prevailed in abundance in the watershed. Brigham Young and other Mormons found ways to irrigate parts of this arid landscape and founded communities that continue to endure. John Wesley Powell explored and mapped the rivers and landforms in the nineteenth century.

The writer Everett Reuss vanished from this landscape as he journeyed through the Colorado Plateau. Many American writers, artists, and musicians have taken great inspiration from this land of infinite hues, whose endless song is expressed by canyon wrens and coyotes.

My late *compañero* and camping partner, author and philosopher Edward Abbey and I trekked for thousands of miles through the Colorado River watershed. No one knew this region better than Abbey. His great lament was the construction of the Glen Canyon Dam that resulted in Lake Powell. Ed wrote twenty-one books, including the great environmental classic *Desert Solitaire* and the well-known novel *The Monkey Wrench Gang*. Many years ago, I recorded one of our conversations wherein Ed Abbey revealed the heart of his philosophy.

EDWARD ABBEY: "By virtue of being alive, we deserve to be respected as individuals. And I am saying that that respect for the value of each human being should be extended to each living thing on the planet. Our fellow creatures, beginning with our pet dogs and cats and horses. Humans find it easy to love them. And we should learn to love the wild animals. The mountain lions, and the rattlesnakes, and coyotes. And developing that way, we extend our ability to love to plant life. I think a tree, a shrub, deserves respect and sympathy as a living thing. And I could even go beyond that, to the rocks, to the air, and to the water. Because it is all part of the whole."

Craig Thompson, who teaches at Western Wyoming Community College in Rock Springs, brings his scientific perspective to the same notion.

CRAIG THOMPSON: "An aquatic ecosystem is the sum total of all of the plants and animals in the watershed—and in the water itself—that depend upon the river. And we especially are concerned about the interactions between these plants and the animals, between the water as it dissolves rocks, and the dissolved products of those are taken up by the plant system, and they begin that food chain. So it is not just looking at the biotic community, the living community and the nonliving community. What we are especially interested in, in an aquatic ecosystem, is the interactions there. Monitoring the system of the exchange of energy and of nutrients in minerals that result in this incredible thing. I mean, I have been fascinated with aquatic ecosystems my entire life."

Bruce Babbitt expressed his heartfelt opinion about both the National Environmental Policy Act (NEPA) and the Endangered Species Act and their effect on development within the Colorado River watershed.

Bruce Babbitt: "NEPA is a remarkable document because it is not a substantive law. It is a process document. But the courts really put teeth in it, in terms of insisting on real processes. This made an enormous difference. It is kind of an affirmation of what real democratic process does. Real democratic process, properly worked, does tend to bring people to their senses. And it has done just that.

"Now, the Endangered Species Act, in contrast, is a substantive law. It sets out a set of criteria, which says, 'Thou shalt not do or take actions which will have the result of endangerment or threat of extinction.' And the Endangered Species Act, during the last ten years particularly, has been a very effective stick on all western rivers. And it has worked. In each case where there has been an endangered species problem, we look back closely into the river system and see that there is a lot of water sloshing around being inefficiently used, and we can redesign uses and revive and restore rivers, and protect species in the process."

Neither the National Environmental Policy Act nor the Endangered Species Act had come into effect when Edward Abbey wrote *The Monkey Wrench Gang*. It was this novel that inspired a new generation of environmentalists to take activism seriously. This novel also focused, in part, on the Glen Canyon Dam, and has instigated a growing movement to decommission this dam so that the Colorado River might again run wild, at least as far as Lake Mead. Attorney Pam Hyde is in the vanguard of those who would see the dam decommissioned.

Pam Hyde: "It is the 1922 Colorado River Compact that really caused the upper basin to push for the construction of Glen Canyon Dam. If we hadn't had the compact with the split at Lee's Ferry, with a delivery requirement right there, there wouldn't have necessarily been a need to create storage just upstream from there. But the upper-basin states went, 'Wow, as long as we have got this delivery requirement, we need to have some way to assure that even in dry years we have got the means to meet that delivery requirement. Let's build a storage facility just upstream of the dividing point.' Now we have got a huge reservoir in the middle of the desert that evaporates a huge amount of water off the top, which doesn't make sense when you have a limited amount of water. Why should we be losing hundreds of thousands of acre-feet to evaporation? If we could go back and eliminate that split, eliminate the delivery requirement, have some other way of allocating and sharing the water, you might completely eliminate the need to have these huge storage facilities."

The late Luna Leopold is regarded as one of the great hydrologists of all time. It was he who first published the American classic *Sand County Almanac*, which was written by his father, Aldo Leopold. Luna had interesting comments about reservoir evaporation.

LUNA LEOPOLD: "The evaporation losses from Lake Mead are about 5 percent of the average inflow to the lake, or about 700,000 to 900,000 acre-feet per year. The soluble salts from the evaporated water are left in the lake. So you are losing 700,000 to 900,000 acre-feet per year from Lake Mead alone. There is not much difference between Lake Mead and Lake Powell."

In other words, about 10 percent of the annual yield of the Colorado River is lost to evaporation from the surfaces of Lake Mead and Lake Powell. That is equivalent to almost twice the amount of New Mexico's annual allocation, and five times that of Nevada! During times of drought such as the Southwest is experiencing at the time of writing, the loss of that much water to evaporation is nearly catastrophic. In the early twentieth century, the Bureau of Reclamation was instrumental for setting parameters as to what was to be legally considered as "best use." Agriculture won the day, and thus the great irrigation districts along the lower Colorado River were to be the greatest recipients of water. Coupled with Samuel P. Hays's "gospel of efficiency," the "best use" policy was put into effect with no regard for the Colorado River itself. It was anticipated early on that the human population of California would grow enormously. Now, in this time of drought, it becomes ever-more obvious that when put into practice, the gospel of efficiency is vastly incomplete as a point of view. It demonstrates the rut of linear thinking that our culture has fallen into. We dangle the carrot of economic prosperity before the eye of the collective mind and fail to perceive the myriad ramifications of what we do as we pursue growth for the sake of growth. Ultimately we find ourselves high and dry, beached on the bank of the devastating rut we have hewn through our paradise, a rut we have legitimized through congressional legislation known as the Law of the River.

In 2001, Don Pope was the manager of the Yuma County Water Users Association, which claims senior rights to about one-third of Arizona's entitlement to the Colorado River. Here he shares his perspective regarding the importance of this entitlement to the people of Yuma.

DON POPE: "The state of Arizona has 2.8 million acre-feet of entitlement on the Colorado. And of that 2.8 million acre-feet, we happen to have, approximately, right at one-third of that here in the Yuma area. It is the senior one-third. So we consider it pretty much a drought-proof allocation. And that amount of water here makes us a $1 billion-plus agriculture industry here in Yuma. Yuma is the winter lettuce capitol of the country. Between Thanksgiving and Easter, the full 75 percent and oftentimes as much as 90 percent of the iceberg lettuce consumed in this country comes from Yuma."

The farmers of the Imperial Irrigation District, on the west side of the river, are working diligently to find means of conserving water. This district receives the lion's share of California's apportionment of 4.4 million acre-feet annually. When I interviewed him in 2001, Rudy Maldonado was the president of the board of directors of Division Six of the Imperial Irrigation District. He tells us of irrigation conservation methods that are used in his district.

RUDY MALDONADO: "Well, there are different irrigation methods. We can use drip irrigation, and we do that quite a bit now. There is dead-level irrigation, where they level the field so there is absolutely no runoff. But that takes money to do that. Then you have pump-back systems, where you have pumps at the end of the field that will collect the water in the reservoir and pump it back to the beginning of the field. And then there are combinations of other ways to irrigate. You know, our farmers are pretty creative. We wanted to get the input from the farmers because they were the ones that would have to implement these processes to make up the conserved water. Again, our farmers will really determine what methods will be used to conserve that water."

The coastal cities of California rely more and more on the Colorado River for their water. Both the Metropolitan Water District of Los Angeles and the San Diego County Water Authority are purchasing water from the irrigation districts of the lower Colorado River. Historian and author Norris Hundley revealed a great deal about these water transfers.

NORRIS HUNDLEY: "The Metropolitan Water District [MWD] of California has an agreement with the Imperial Valley for about 100,000 acre-feet. MWD also has agreements with central valley agencies—some of them in the Central Valley Project, some of them not part of the Central Valley Project—for transfer of agricultural water to cities. There are some restrictions. The law makes some restrictions on this sort of thing. But a determined seller and the determined buyer have been able to work these sorts of things out to date. And what is the incentive? Why are farmers wanting to do this? It is very simple. It is money. For example, the Imperial Irrigation District pays the Bureau of Reclamation roughly $40 an acre-foot for water, for which it can get $249 an acre-foot. Transfers of water from agriculture to cities has some potential serious by-products. The farmers succumb to this in a major way. You are going to see the disappearance of open spaces. You are going to see the disappearance of agriculture. You are going to see the intensification of urban sprawl. And some University of California scientists recently released a report which indicated that within a decade and a half, two decades, that the central valley is going to consist of a series of large cities surrounded by virtually nonexistent agricultural enclaves, covered overhead by smog, all the way from Bakersfield to north of Sacramento."

In a very real sense agriculturists are competing with developing cities for the precious waters of the Colorado River. The great irrigation projects are withering in the face of the shift from agrarian to urban economics. Ethnobotanist and author Gary Paul Nabhan is a great critic of these modern trends.

GARY PAUL NABHAN: "One interesting thing that you bring up is this competition between urban areas and agricultural areas for water. And I think it is one of the greatest fallacies that has been put forth in the public arena, that for years we learned that Arizona was first using 90 percent of its water for agriculture, and then 85 percent, and then by some analysis is now down to 80 percent. And that it [agriculture] was incredibly wasteful, and we should make agriculture get more efficient, and allow more of that water to be used 'democratically' by the people in urban areas. So now Phoenix and Yuma and other towns in the Colorado River bottomlands have now expanded grossly into the most fertile, irrigable lands in Arizona. When you look at the water use per unit acre for a hundred acres of condominium development, and say that that use of water is going to continue to grow, or at least be maintained near that level because the condominiums are not going to go away— that land will never come back to agriculture. Water use per unit acre is much, much higher for urban use than agricultural use and offers none of the environmental amenities in terms of open space, or cleaning the air, or wildlife habitat that healthy agriculture could offer. Originally the Central Arizona Project planned to help Arizona farmers. And now most of its transfer of waters is clearly being used to fuel urban growth rather than promote a healthier agricultural system."

Patricia Mulroy finds great hope in the recently developed practice of water banking, wherein water is pumped cross-country from the Colorado River and deposited in lake beds where the water is intended to seep back into overmined aquifers in Arizona where it can be stored for future use.

PATRICIA MULROY: "What I really like about the water-banking arrangement is it forms partnerships. It creates mutual futures, not individual futures. The Colorado River is a mutual future. And it starts binding and bringing together benefits and consequences. We don't mind paying the money. I mean, it is going to cost us $170 million to $180 million. But we know that we are not paying any profit or any markup. We are paying what it costs. The state of Arizona shouldn't have to pay for us. We are paying our fair share. And we are paying what it costs to bank the water, and we are paying what it costs to retrieve the water. They have the benefit of the environmental restoration, because the water is going into the ground. They have the benefit of it helping their water-management picture in the state of Arizona. And we [Nevada] have a future supply of water in the state of Arizona, and if times get tough, we have a drought bank to where we can mitigate the consequences of a drought here in this urban area."

For years, California has been pumping far more than its share of Colorado River water. In his final days as secretary of the interior, water master Bruce Babbitt demanded that California get back in line with its annual apportionment of 4.4 million acre-feet as defined in the 1922 Colorado River Compact. Ed Marston is the publisher of *High Country News*, one of the most informative publications to come out of the intermountain west.

ED MARSTON: "Over Babbitt's eight years in office, he, with the help of other people and under pressure from the other Colorado River states, encouraged, forced, cajoled California to agree over the next fifteen years or so to skinny their use down to 4.4 million acre-feet. In return for that, California got a guarantee that it would have enough water, no matter what the weather did, to get it through the next fifteen years—that it wouldn't be cut off, as it could be legally—and that extra water will come out of the 56 million acre-feet that is being stored in lakes Mead and Powell. In other words, if there is a drought, the other states and the federal government have agreed that they will draw those reservoirs down far enough to keep California in water."

BRUCE BABBITT: "The California problem goes back a long way. So basically, the other basin states, not using their draw, California [is] expanding, metastasizing like crazy, sucking up the water—really kind of threatening to blow up the compact arrangements. And what we said to California was, 'We have got to resolve this in the framework of the 1922 Colorado River Compact. You have got to reduce your draw.' And the way to get more water these days is not more dams, not more reclamation projects. It is efficiency in water transfers from agriculture to urban. And you, California, have a lake, an ocean of water sitting out there in the Imperial Valley. It is the oldest rights on the Colorado River. It is several million acre-feet a year. There is plenty of water, if we will just get down to the business of the economics of transfers. It took some pressure. We had to go back and really lean hard on them. But it is done, and I think it is a model for how we find water in the future. We can find it through efficiencies and transfers."

There is a growing movement of environmentally conscious people on either side of the international boundary who are seeking water to restore the delta of the Colorado River. For many years, almost no water has reached the Sea of Cortés. The result is that the ecosystem of the delta has been deeply wounded. Many species are now endangered. Many fishing communities are also endangered. Dale Pontius is an attorney and Colorado River scholar. He addressed the international movement to restore the delta.

DALE PONTIUS: "People who have been working on ecological issues on the border, and particularly in northern Mexico have felt for years that there wasn't anything in the 1944 treaty with Mexico that dealt with ecological issues. Obviously, in those days, people didn't think about it. And they wanted to have something in the way of an amendment to that treaty that would start a process whereby the two countries could begin to develop ideas and, hopefully, a program that could be implemented to restore and protect the fragile ecology in the delta, south of the border. And there had been growing pressure from the coalition of nonprofits, conservation groups in Mexico, and certainly with a lot of input and leadership from the U.S. side. And they have formed quite a coalition. And they have started to have an impact in terms of the Mexican government becoming aware of these issues. Particularly the new administration of Mexico seems to be very sensitive to this. And they have made overtures directly to this government from that administration saying, 'It is time we dealt with this issue.' And Secretary Babbitt at his last speech to the Colorado River users said, 'The big unfinished business item on the Colorado River is the restoration of the delta.'"

Elena Cheverilla and her husband, Carlos Valdez Casillas, were in the vanguard of the environmental movement in Sonora, Mexico, for many years. Elena speaks of the participation of nongovernmental organizations (NGOs) in urging the government to move forward.

ELENA CHEVERILLA: "The law has changed—the environment law. NGOs are working closer to the government. But I still don't see serious commitment. I would like to see more of that. And certainly I am not that kind of Mexican who will say, 'This is all a blame of the government.' It is only a reflection of us as citizens."

Steve Cornelius is a biologist and the former director of the Sonoran Institute. His research focused on ecological requirements for restoration of the delta.

STEVE CORNELIUS: "We need to have some better understanding, frankly, of what we are talking about when we say we need to restore the delta. Until that geographic scope of restoration has been defined and agreed to amongst all of us who are expected to contribute to its restoration, it is going to be very difficult to agree on how much water is really needed, and what its quality is, what its periodicity is on the flows. And especially it is going to be very difficult to identify the sources for that water."

BRUCE BABBITT: "Anyone who has ever read Aldo Leopold's essay about camping and canoeing in that delta prior to Hoover Dam will never have the same view of what we did to the Colorado River. And I think for years people said, 'Well, it is beyond hope of ever restoring.' What we have done in the last four or five years is started to rethink that. I have had a lot of conversations with the former Mexican environment minister. She began raising the issue of doing all this restoration all over the United States. 'What about this salt flat that used to be this lush wonderful delta?' And we began talking about it. We set in motion some study groups. And they are coming back saying that a relatively small amount of water could revitalize and restore a significant part of that delta. And what we now need to do is keep those discussions going, recognize that we have an existing block of water in the Welton–Mohawk drain, which is already going into the delta, and which must be preserved as a delta block, and that we can in fact free up some additional water. People say, 'Where?' What I say in response is, 'From a lot of different sources where the water is currently being wasted and not wisely used.' "

The Welton–Mohawk drain is agricultural runoff water that has a higher salinity content than the Colorado River, and as such has too much salt to be further used by farmers in Mexico. Irrigation leads to salinization of fresh water. Subsequently, about 135,000 acre-feet of Welton–Mohawk water actually now drains into the eastern area of the delta, and the ecology has revitalized to an amazing degree. During years when drought is not a problem, water can indeed be spared, as Bruce Babbitt suggests, to follow its natural course to the delta and resurrect this formerly lush ecosystem that for many decades has been a dead zone.

In December 2007, Secretary of the Interior Dirk Kempthorne signed a water pact that allows for adjustments in water allocation as earlier specified by the Colorado River Compact of 1922. The lower-basin states will share the impact of predicted water shortages. Urban growth is gaining the upper hand over agriculture, and the handwriting on the wall is that as the Sunbelt cities continue to grow, agriculturalists will be paid to relinquish their prior claim to the river. The concept of "best use" is shifting from agriculture to urban growth. The fact that global warming is upon us has an enormous impact on the American Southwest. It is thought that by the end of the twenty-first century, annual precipitation may diminish by 25 to 30 percent. Snowpack will likely decrease, and the current drought that has lasted for eight years may well last for many more.

Pipelines are being considered to deliver water from northern to southern Nevada where the Las Vegas area is presently the fastest-growing urban center in America. Northern Nevada ranchers are opposed to this transfer of water from their ranchlands where the springs are already running low.

Las Vegas will draw a greater share from Lake Mead in return for financing a reservoir in California to collect water that would otherwise have gone to Mexico in excess of their treaty allocation of 1.5 million acre-feet a year.

Just north of the boundary with Mexico, a desalination plant constructed fifteen years ago that has sat idle is now to be put into use to remove salt buildup in the Colorado River that occurs as a by-product of irrigation.

At the time of writing, both Lake Mead and Lake Powell are about half full—as low as they have been since 1973.

Little thought is being given to ecological concerns. One could extrapolate a very real possibility that as the human population of the Southwest grows and grows and grows, there will come a moment of reckoning when the precarious stability of the environment will collapse, lakes Mead and Powell will dry up, and scientists will be at a loss as to how to fix the problem. Then what?

It seems to me that leading the reckless charge of the Four Horsemen of the Apocalypse is human overpopulation. In collective response to both a biblical apothegm and our steaming biological urges, we have gone forth and fructified ourselves to the edge of the abyss.

In 1970, I read a most provocative essay entitled "The Tragedy of the Commons," to me a lucid post-Malthusian document that addresses human overpopulation. It was published in 1968 by Garrett Hardin, a human ecologist who taught for many years at the University of California at Santa Barbara. I visited Dr. Hardin at his home in a rural area north of Santa Barbara where I recorded our conversation as we ate fresh strawberries. He reiterated his thinking about his essay.

GARRETT HARDIN: "It's a very simple idea, almost simpleminded. I took as the example the historical instance of common pasturelands in England, which were called 'commons,' and pointed out that those worked very well, probably for hundreds of years. Then along toward the seventeenth and eighteenth centuries, people became aware of the fact that something was wrong—that the commons were being overgrazed and consequently they were going downhill. The basic reason was that when people have access to common lands on the basis of their need as they perceive it, and when the population grows to the point where the number of people exceeds the carrying capacity of the land, or the number of cows exceeds the carrying capacity of the pasture, then each person, seeking his own self-interest, will put the number of cows he wants to on the common pastureland. The result is that presently there are too many, and the whole thing is destroyed.

"Now the reason that this is a tragedy is because even after each individual realizes what is happening, he is powerless to stop it, because he says, 'Well, if I don't get it, the pigs will.' In other words, my neighbors, who are pigs, will get it. So I'll take mine before the pigs get theirs. Each neighbor reasons in the same way. Although there's complete knowledge of what is happening, the deterioration is inevitable. So this is like a Greek tragedy where knowledge doesn't prevent the unfortunate end. There is an escape from this, of course, and that is to get rid of the commons. Then you have two possibilities. Either you can turn it into private property, as was done in England (unjustly, I may say, the way it was done, but at least this will save the pastureland). Or you can turn it into public property, and then you have to appoint managers. And then you're at the mercy of the managers. If they manage well, it's fine; but if they don't, it isn't good. So there's no simple answer as to which one of the other systems will work better—private property (privatism) or socialism. Either one may work, or either one may not work. But the one clear thing is that the commons cannot possibly work once the population has become too great.

"The Colorado River is indeed the fragile aquatic lifeline of much of the American West and northwestern Mexico. It serves a burgeoning human population of more than 25 million of us, who rely on these waters for our very subsistence. It also serves all of our other fellow species, on whom we rely and who rely on us to maintain balance in our home environment.

I asked my old friend the poet and philosopher Gary Snyder to "think like a watershed."

GARY SNYDER: "Watersheds are obvious concepts to think in terms of. They have unarguable boundaries, and they are easy to map. They are a very clear entity in the phenomenal world. A lot of watershed thinking is very professional, scientific, organized and led by government agencies, in many cases, and the territory and hydrologists and GIS [geographic information system] mappers, soil scientists, fisheries people, and so forth. But there is another side that actually goes back several decades, which is the community watershed consciousness, where people became engaged with their watershed regions as part of reinhabitation, of becoming members of a place, of part of a decision to become a people who live somewhere, and who take responsibility for a place as members of that community. That is the cultural side of what we call bioregionalism. And that has brought about watershed groups and watershed consciousness, which is not simply measuring the rate of flow or testing pollution, but is writing poems. It is painting pictures, taking photographs, telling tales. Watershed art. And watershed celebrations, Like Lewis MacAdams and his Friends of the Los Angeles River started before anything else with a river celebration for the L.A. River. Everybody thought they were nuts. Celebrate that old ditch? Lewis said, 'We have got to start somewhere. Let's do a dance, and read poems to cheer it up.' That is actually how it started. To cheer the river up. If one is professional, you are thinking about it like E. O. Wilson thinks about life in a way. If you are a community member, all the qualities of the region, including its beauty and its integrity, are part of what concern you. And you don't measure the watershed simply in nuts-and-bolts terms of biological diversity and soil quality, or water purity. But in something that is subtler and deeper, which is: 'How does it feel? How is life doing here? How are things all getting along with each other? What kind of a dance is this? How is the soul doing? How is the music rising from it? How do we feel when we walk the ridge or go down the river?' Insights and feelings that come out of that are expressed in the arts. They are also expressed in architecture. They are expressed in the designs you put on your shirt and the kinds of sandals you wear. They enter in ways that we can't even quite trace. They enter into the life of the place of the people who live in the place. That is true."

WILLIAM DEBUYS: "The most powerful thing about watershed units from a governance perspective is that if we organized ourselves politically, watershed by watershed, we would be [organized] in groups that possessed interrelated interests. The people at the top of the watershed affect the people at the bottom of the watershed. Therefore the people at the bottom of the watershed have an interest in the resources at the top of the watershed. And people would be unified instead of our present arrangement of being so fragmented, county by county, or in politics that are too big to think bioregionally, which the state of New Mexico certainly is. We wind up divided by the conflicts in our interests rather than unified by the interrelation of our interests. And a watershed is a natural unit for interrelated interests. Because everything that goes on in the watershed affects the water quality that the people in that geographic region depend on."

The watersheds of the American West are the sites of the most rapidly growing urban centers in America. They are also home to many of the wilderness areas that remain in the coterminous United States. My old friend Melissa Savage is a biogeographer and director of the Four Corners Institute in Santa Fe. She has devoted much of her life to preservation of wildlife habitats and wilderness areas where biodiversity flourishes, and without which life as we know it would be impoverished. I recorded a conversation with Melissa as we looked at a map of New Mexico that identified proposed wilderness areas.

MELISSA SAVAGE: "Wilderness is a place where the human touch has been very light. I think it is quite desirable to say these are places where we can close the roads. And the main message about natural places is that we are losing them. And losing them. And losing them. People are busy in their own lives, and just don't have the time and the energy to pay attention to what is happening. And what is happening is extremely serious globally. And it is extremely serious in New Mexico. We are losing species. We are losing viable water systems. We are losing forest systems. We are losing grasslands. You know, every natural community has lost so much of its area, and even places that are semi-wild have lost so much quality that we can't afford to lose any more. And there is this movement in the West to retain the very last scraps. Most natural areas have to be pretty big chunks in order to retain the species of animals, for example, that need room to move around. A thousand acres is not enough for many mammal species. So we are at a very critical time, I think. And if these last scraps don't get put into some kind of wilderness area now, we will never have them again. They are gone forever.

"There have been over geologic time five gigantic species-extinction episodes. For example, we can document that at one time 96 percent of marine species went extinct, a fairly catastrophic event for life on Earth. But we are now in the middle of the sixth giant catastrophic species loss, and it is completely due to human activities. Most people can't relate to that. You read these articles in the newspaper, and it becomes part of the background of the terrible things that are happening everywhere. But this is completely irreversible. We can probably reverse many things, but we cannot reverse species loss. It takes millions of years for diversity to recover.

"So this little map of proposed wilderness areas [in New Mexico] with its boundary lines drawn in may seem like some kind of political struggle. It is not just a political struggle. I believe that the single most important thing happening in the West right now is the protection of the remaining [wilderness] areas. Most of our wilderness right now is rock and ice. It is in high-elevation areas that nobody has wanted to claim, where it is easier to designate wilderness. And a lot of these areas proposed for protection are at low elevation. They are riparian areas. They are grasslands. They are communities at low elevation, so they have had a lot of impact. These areas are absolutely critical to the species that remain. So without them, those species will just go. And we will see it soon, in twenty years, ten years. We will see them go. So that is why I think it is really important to make these wilderness proposals happen, not only in New Mexico but throughout the West."

Within the context of geologic time, political boundaries are ephemeral, recently rendered, likely soon to vanish. One of life's greatest urges is to feel rooted in homeland, to know its seasons, its fellow biota, its horizons, its watersheds. My great friend Enrique Lamadrid joined the human species from within the Río Grande watershed. His sense of homeland is profound.

Enrique Lamadrid: "There is an extraordinary sense of cultural homeland. We call it querencia. Querencia is a folk concept, it's a sense of belonging, it's a sense of rootedness. Querencia is the place where you know you belong. Sometimes it's the place where you were born. It's mobile, you can develop a new querencia in a new place. But how do you set down roots in a new place? There are many ways of doing that, of becoming part of a new place. And people certainly did it here. People who are from New Mexico want to be in New Mexico. If they're not here, they're trying to figure out how to come home. Querencia means all of those things. It comes from the verb querer, to want or to love. It's a place that you love, a place that you want to be, that even has a sense of the place you want to die in."

WILLIAM DEBUYS: "I think that this idea of just somehow all of us becoming native to whatever place we pick to be and staying that way is a huge challenge. And I see wilderness as central to that. Because whatever background we come from, we try to become native to our place, to renew our native-ness. Where do we touch the benchmark of what that place is? Where can we do that better than in wilderness? And without wilderness, I would feel, myself personally, as though my compass didn't work. Wilderness is the place where you get calibrated to the land so that both literally and figuratively you can get your bearings. And without getting your bearings, you can never become native to anything."

For those of us who have had the good fortune to run wild rivers, hike mountain trails, camp in remote corners of desert country far from urban environments, look at the lay of the land with a mind to "thinking like a watershed," there is a profound sense of restoration in motion. Nothing is static. The very planet is a living organism with an enveloping consciousness of its own. And if we void our individual minds of the frenetic overlay that dominates much of day-to-day consciousness, and open up to the flow of Nature, clarity and balance come to prevail. Or such has been my experience.

And at every dawn and every dusk I thank the spirit of Nature for this span of consciousness that is my lifetime.

A Hopi Prophecy,
as Spoken by Hopi Elders

     SHORTLY AFTER NOON on March 16, 1971, an old Hopi Indian man whose eyes stared sightlessly through the light of the noonday sun was guided by his friend to the stairs that led to the top of a kiva, or ceremonial chamber, at Hotevilla. Old David Monongye mounted the stairs and stood on the roof of the ancient ceremonial chambers and shouted clearly across the nearby rooftops that there was to be a meeting of the elders in the kiva. David asked me to accompany him into the underground kiva, a long rectangular room built within the Earth and lighted only by the sun's rays that passed through the ceremonial opening in the roof.

In the middle of the room stood an old woodstove. David easily found his way to a wood box beside the stove and selected several pieces of juniper that he placed inside the stove and lit into a warming fire. He then went to a receptacle containing old stone ceremonial pipes, one of which he selected and filled with Indian tobacco from a leather pouch. Contemplatively he smoked, and with each puff sent his prayers to the Great Spirit.

One by one, elderly Hopi men from Hotevilla and neighboring Oraibi drifted into the kiva. They included Thomas Banyacya—appointed interpreter for the traditional Hopis, whose face was a weary record of the months he had spent traveling through America pleading with anyone who would listen that Black Mesa should remain unmolested by the Peabody Coal Company—and at least two dozen others, all ancient and dignified.

John Lansa—husband of Mina Lansa, the *kikmongwi* of Oraibi—rose and spoke for many minutes in the gentle tones of his Hopi language. Occasionally his words were emphasized by several low-pitched grunts of affirmation from the assembled elders.

As John spoke, Thomas and others roasted small cornmeal tamales on top of the woodstove. When the tamales were cooked, they put them on the floor for anyone to help himself. They were sweet and good and the corn had been ground by hand using *manos* and *metates*.

When John had finished speaking, Thomas turned to me and said, "It is very difficult to translate John's words into English because Hopi is much different than English. You can say things in Hopi that no words can say in English. This is because Hopis think different from the whites.

"Anyway, I will try to tell you what John says. He says that what you call Mother Earth is everything important to the Hopis. It is the land, all living things, the water, the trees, the rocks—it is everything. It is the force or the power that comes from these things that keeps the world together.

"We sit here in the kiva which is the womb of the Earth. This kiva is our church and our school. Here in the kiva is where our leaders work. In here we have our ceremonials, here in the Earth so that Nature will work in harmony with the people. When we have ceremonials, this keeps the natural forces together.

"A long time ago, many generations before the white men came, the Great Spirit came to this place. He was the first one to come here. The Hopis asked permission from him to come and live here. The Great Spirit told the Hopis they could live here but they would have to follow the rules and live according to his teaching. The Hopis said they would, and asked the Great Spirit to be their leader. The Great Spirit said that the Hopis had to have their own leaders.

"The Great Spirit told the Hopis that this place here is the spiritual center of this land. This is the most sacred place, right here in this mesa. This is where the Hopis must pray. They must pray for all things on this continent because this is the spiritual center.

"The Hopis pray for balance so that all things will be well and healthy. The Hopis remember today what the Great Spirit first told them long ago. The leaders pass it down and teach the young people what the Great Spirit first taught the Hopis. This is better than writing it down because this way we all know what the Great Spirit first told us.

"Before the white men came, all the Hopis were happy and sang all the time. Every morning, the people get up at dawn and run to the springs and bathe in cold water. This makes our hearts strong. Then the people run home and eat breakfast. After they eat, the people run to gardens and work all day long. After they work all day in their gardens, the people run home. All the time they are running, the people are singing. Everyone was happy in those days. After they get home and eat their dinner, the people weave or have ceremonials. All the time, people were singing.

"The Hopis don't have any class structures at all—no bosses, no policemen, no judges—everyone was equal. No one had more than he needed. There weren't any politics, then. Everyone lived together in harmony. We have a chief [*kikmongwi*] who helps us remember the words of the Great Spirit, and people help the chief in the ceremonials. We have many ceremonials so everything stays in balance with Nature.

"In those days the air was clear and everyone could see far. We always look to the Earth Mother for food and nourishment. We never take more than we need. Our lives were very rich and humble. We live close to the Earth as laid out by the Great Spirit.

"When the white men came, everything started to get out of balance. The white brother has no spiritual knowledge, only technical. He made the white man's government, which always try to take away the Indian's land. For a long time the government and the bureau [of Indian Affairs] not try to take our land because nobody wanted it. It is very dry here and only Indians know how to live on this land. The Great Spirit taught the Hopis how to live on this land.

"Then in 1935 or so, the bureau convince a few people to have a tribal council. Almost no one wanted it. Only a few people who had been educated in the bureau school and learned the white man's ways. All of them who are on the tribal council are Christians, either Mormons or Mennonites, and they have forgotten the Hopi religion.

"Now the bureau has made schools here and they make our children go to those schools. The children don't get to learn the Hopi way. It takes a lifetime to learn the Hopi way. This is the way the government is trying to conquer the Hopi way. It tries to divide the people and confuse them.

"Then the Hopi Tribal Council signed a contract with the Peabody Coal Company to come up here to Black Mesa and take away the coal. The Hopi people don't know about this. The tribal council does this for the money. Clarence

Hamilton is [at the time this was spoken] the chairman of the tribal council. What he did was illegal. The Hopi people didn't even know about the contract for a long time. And then the Peabody Coal Company was already on Black Mesa.

"Now there is a big strip mine where coal comes out of the Earth to send electricity to the big cities. This makes upheaval on the land. They cut across our sacred shrines and destroy prayers to the six directions. Our prayers go in all directions for everything so that there will be balance. We are not to use the Earth in a way that is destructive.

"Peabody is tearing up the land and destroying the sacred mountain. What they take away from our land is being turned into power to create even more evil things. They use these things in war and men fight each other. The Hopis don't believe in the white men's wars. 'Hopi' means peace. The bureau educates our children to the white men's ways and then the government makes them go off to war. We don't want this for our children. It turns them into *kahopis*. *Kahopi* means bad Hopi.

"Peabody is taking water away from this land. We pray that the rains come so we will have good crops. It is very bad that Peabody takes away the water because it upsets the balance of things. You can't do things like that and have Nature be in balance. The white men don't understand this.

"When they burn the coal, it fills the sky with poison gases. This will hurt the growing things. Peabody is polluting the watershed. All of this will make upheaval.

"The Hopi prophecies are drawn on a rock on Black Mesa. The prophecy says there will come a time of much destruction. This is the time. The prophecy says there will be paths in the sky. The paths are airplanes. There will be cobwebs in the air. These are the power lines. Great ashes will be dumped on cities and there will be destruction. These are the atom bombs America dropped on Hiroshima [and Nagasaki]. The prophecy says men will travel to the moon and stars and this will cause disruption and the time of the great purification will be very near. It is bad that spacemen brought things back from the moon. That is very bad. The Great Spirit says that man will not go any further when he builds a city in the sky. When that happens, the great purification will come next.

"The Great Spirit says that the Hopis will be the only ones left who remember the truth and even they will be confused. But if they live according to Nature here at the spiritual center of the continent, they will survive the great purification. The Hopis are to try and tell people how to live, and then each person will decide if he will be a good person or a bad person. The bad people will all be destroyed. Many of them will just die of fright. That is why the Hopis bathe in cold water every morning—to keep their hearts strong. It will really be very bad at the time of the great purification.

"The Hopis know that you can't treat Nature the way that Peabody is or something will happen. There will be a time of many earthquakes or droughts or floods. Many people will get sick and die. The Hopis know this because the Great Spirit told them.

"The Great Spirit said, 'I was the first—I will be the last.' "

AUDIO CD

Healing the West: Voices of Culture and Habitat Sound Collage

Written, narrated, and produced by Jack Loeffler in the Peregrine Arts studio.

1. Jack Loeffler (JL): Introduction
2. Mylie Lawyer, Nez Percé: Coyote Story
3. Ed Edmo and Sophie George: Coyote Stories
4. Allen Pinkham, Nez Percé: Creation
5. Allen Pinkham, Nez Percé: Preservation of Habitat
6. Sharon Dick, Yakima: Salmon Lifeway
7. JL: Damming of Columbia River, Ed Edmo, Shoshone-Bannock
8. Jamie Pinkham, Nez Percé: Sense of Habitat
9. JL: Human Presence Along the Río Grande
10. Rina Swentzell, Santa Clara: Water, Wind, Breath
11. Dolores Lewis, Acoma Potter
12. Gary Paul Nabhan: Re-storying the Land, Song of Canyonlands
13. Vernon Masayesva, Hopi: Emergence, Pact with Massau
14. Vernon Masayesva, Hopi: Preserve or Perish; Annie Kahn, Navajo: POV
15. Roy Kady, Navajo: Origin of Sheep; Gibson Gonnie, Singer
16. Roberta Blackgoat, Navajo: Won't Be Relocated
17. JL: About the Central Arizona Project
18. Shonto Begay, Navajo: "Grandfather's Thoughts Are Disturbed"
19. Patty Limerick, Historian: From Verdant East to Arid West
20. JL: About the Colorado River
21. William deBuys, Author: Salton Sea, Plumbing the Colorado
22. William Swan, Water Attorney: Colorado River Compact
23. Stewart Udall: California Gets Lion's Share of Colorado River
24. David Brower: Environmentalist's Look at Economics
25. Garrett Hardin: Tragedy of the Commons
26. Daniel Kemmis: Politics and Place
27. Gary Snyder: Watershed/Bioregional Thinking
28. Edward Abbey: The Total Egalitarian
29. Camillus Lopez, Tohono O'odham: Song of Frog Mountain
30. JL: Homeland; Enrique Lamadrid: *Querencia*
31. Chuy Martinez: Indita del Río Grande
32. Song of the Sandhill Cranes
33. Chorus of Elk and Coyote
34. Dawn Voice of the Sonoran

© 2008 Jack Loeffler